A HISTORY OF
THE AMERICAN PEOPLE

BY

WOODROW WILSON, Ph.D., Litt.D., LL.D.

IN FIVE VOLUMES

Vol. I.

The Swarming of the English

Woodrow Wilson

A HISTORY OF
THE AMERICAN PEOPLE

BY

WOODROW WILSON, Ph.D., Litt.D., LL.D.

PRESIDENT OF THE UNITED STATES

ILLUSTRATED WITH PORTRAITS, MAPS
PLANS, FACSIMILES, RARE PRINTS
CONTEMPORARY VIEWS, ETC.

IN FIVE VOLUMES

Vol. I.

NEW YORK AND LONDON
HARPER & BROTHERS PUBLISHERS

TO

E. A. W.

IN LOVING ACKNOWLEDGMENT OF GENTLE

BENEFITS WHICH CAN NEITHER BE

MEASURED NOR REPAID

CONTENTS

NOTES ON ILLUSTRATIONS

NOTES ON ILLUSTRATIONS

NOTES ON ILLUSTRATIONS

NOTES ON ILLUSTRATIONS

NOTES ON ILLUSTRATIONS

NOTES ON ILLUSTRATIONS

NOTES ON ILLUSTRATIONS

NOTES ON ILLUSTRATIONS

NOTES ON ILLUSTRATIONS

NOTES ON ILLUSTRATIONS

NOTES ON ILLUSTRATIONS

NOTES ON ILLUSTRATIONS

NOTES ON ILLUSTRATIONS

NOTES ON ILLUSTRATIONS

NOTES ON ILLUSTRATIONS

---

*For the verification of the documents and the illustrative
material here, and for the notes on their sources, we are in-
debted to Mr. Victor H. Paltsits, of the New York Public
Library (Lenox Building), whose scholarly researches made
possible so full a list.*

A HISTORY OF
THE AMERICAN PEOPLE

A HISTORY OF
THE AMERICAN PEOPLE

CHAPTER I

BEFORE THE ENGLISH CAME

WHEN the history of English settlement in America begins, the breathless, eager stir of the Elizabethan age is over, and the sober, contentious seventeenth century has come, with its perplexed politics, its schismatic creeds, its scheming rivalries in trade. An age of discovery and bold adventure has given place to an age of commerce and organization. More than one hundred years have elapsed since the discovery of North America. Spain has lost her great place in the politics of Europe, and France and England are pressing forward to take it. While parts changed and the stage was reset, the century through, the great continent lay "a veiled and virgin shore," inflaming desires that could not be gratified, stirring dreams that only enticed brave men to their death, exciting to enterprise and adventure, but never to substantial or lasting achievement. The same mistake that had led to its discovery had prevented its profitable occupation. Columbus had set out to seek, not a new continent, but old Cathay; and died believing that what he had found was in fact the eastern coasts of Asia. The explorers who followed him in the next century had persisted in seeking, as he had sought, not new, but old lands, rich with ancient kingdoms and fabled stores of treasure, lying ready to the hand of conqueror and buccaneer. Such ancient kingdoms Cortez and Pizarro actually found in South America and upon the Isthmus; and such every adventurer promised himself he should find just beyond the coasts of the northern continent also. Or else he should find something that would be quite as valuable, and possibly no less romantic,— a fountain of youth, untouched mines of precious ore, or waters floored with priceless pearls.

The discovery of the New World had drawn Europe when she was most credulous into a realm of dreams. The Revival of Learning had come. Europe had read once more and with freshened eyes, as if for the first time, the frank sentences of the ancient classics, written when men looked heartily, fearlessly, artlessly about them, and her imagination had been quickened and enriched by what she read, her thoughts set free and rejuvenated. What she had seen also, as well as what she had read, had given her new life. For the Middle Ages were now passed, and she had herself become a new world. France had lost her feudal princes in the Hundred Years' War, and was at last a real kingdom under veritable kings, for Louis XI. had reigned. England had been transformed by the Wars of the Roses from a feudal into a national monarchy, and the first Tudor was on the throne. Spain had cast out the Moor, and was united under Christian sovereigns. Former geographical relations, too, had disappeared.

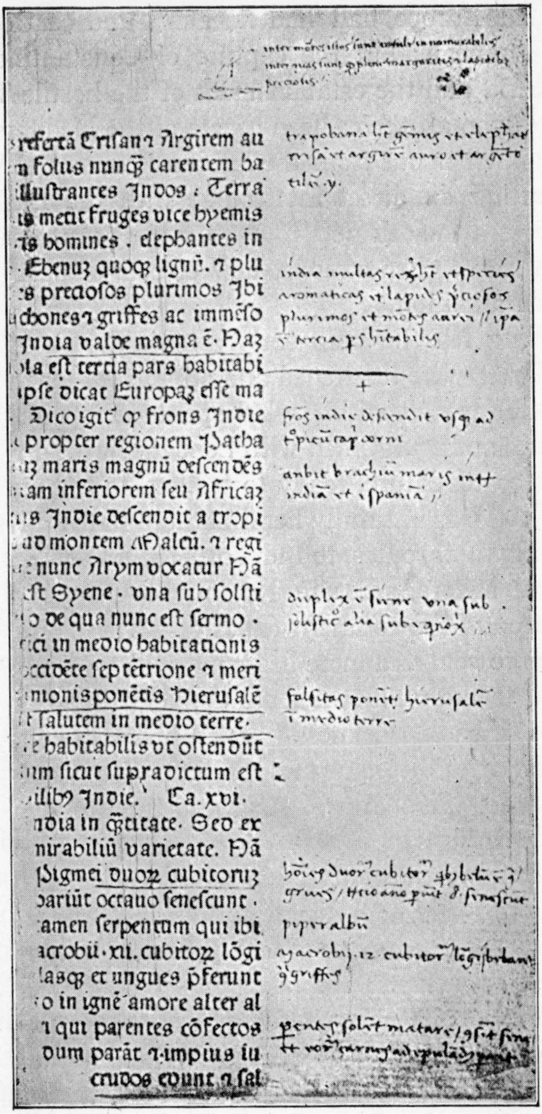

referta Crisan & Argirem au
n folus nunq carentem ba
illustrantes Indos. Terra
is metit fruges vice hyemis
is homines. elephantes in
Ebenuz quoq lignu. & plu
es preciosos plurimos Ibi
dbones & griffes ac immeso
India valde magna e. Naz
ola est tertia pars habitabi
ipse dicat Europaz esse ma
Dico igit q frons Indie
propter regionem Hatha
uz maris magnu descedes
am inferiorem seu Africaz
us Indie descendit a tropi
ad montem Maleu. & regi
nunc Arym vocatur Na
est Syene. vna sub solsti
o de qua nunc est sermo.
ici in medio habitationis
ccidete septetrione & meri
onis ponetis Hierusale
salutem in medio terre.
e habitabilis vt ostendut
um sicut supradictum est
ilibus Indie. Ca. xvi.
ndia in qtitate. Sed ex
nirabiliu varietate. Na
Pigmei duoz cubitoz
pariut octauo senescunt.
amen serpentum qui ibi
acrobii. xii. cubitoz logi
lasq et ungues pferunt
o in igne amore alter al
qui parentes cofectos
dum parat & impius iu
crudos edunt & sal

ANNOTATIONS IN HANDWRITING OF CHRISTOPHER COLUMBUS

The old Europe had had its heart and centre in the Mediterranean; but the capture of Constantinople by the Turk, and the establishment of the hostile Turkish power upon all the eastern coasts of the Mediterranean, now shut her out from the habitual courses of her life by cutting off direct intercourse with the East. She was forced to seek new routes for her commerce, a different life for her nations, new objects of policy, other aims of ambition.

Having felt the keen early airs of the Renaissance, her powers were heartened and stimulated for the task, and she faced it with a glad spontaneity and energy. She was strangely filled with hope and with a romantic ardor for adventure, ready to see and to test every new thing. It was naturally her first thought to find her way again, by new routes, to India and the great East. Portuguese sailors, accordingly, sought and found their way around the southern capes of Africa; and Columbus, more bold and more believing still, pushed straight forth into the unknown Atlantic, that dread and mysterious "Sea of Darkness" which had lain so silent all the centuries, keeping its secrets. He would make directly for the shores of Asia and the kingdom of the Tartars.

In the new delight of giving rein to their imaginations men were ready to believe anything. They could believe even Marco Polo, whom they had hitherto been inclined to deem an impudent impostor. In the latter half of the thirteenth century, Polo, accompanying his father and uncle, had journeyed overland to the farthest kingdoms of Asia, when the great Tartar empire of Kublai Khan stretched from Europe to the Chinese Sea. He had seen throughout nearly twenty years the full splendor of that stupendous realm, its rich provinces, its teeming and ancient cities, its abounding wealth and unexampled power. Some of its authority he had himself wielded; for he had been taken into the intimate counsels of the Great Khan, and had gone up

MARCO POLO

and down his coasts upon weighty errands of state. But the men of his day at home would not credit what he had to tell them of the boundless extent and resplendent glory of lands which no one else among their neighbors had ever seen, or ever heard named even, save by this Venetian adventurer. Who could say what truth there was, or what falsehood, in these tales of the ends

5

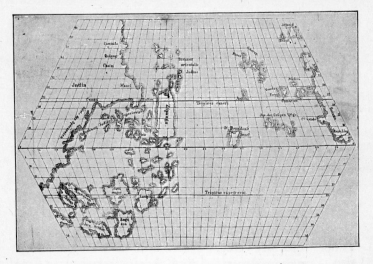

A CONJECTURAL RESTORATION OF TOSCANELLI'S MAP

of Asia and of a great sea lying beyond? Polo's story slumbered, accordingly, in curious manuscripts, or kept covert with the learned, until revived and brought to day again by the congenial air and the enticing credulity of the fifteenth century. In the view of that hopeful age nothing was impossible. These things and many more Columbus credited and pondered, as he pored upon crude and curious maps, sketched out of travellers' tales and astronomers' reckonings; and it was the very Cathay of Marco Polo he put across the new ocean to find.

The success of Columbus solved the mystery of the Atlantic, but it did little to instruct Europe, or even to guide her fancy, concerning the real nature of the lands he had found. No one dreamed that they were the coasts of a new world. Who could believe the globe big enough to have held through all the ages a whole con-

tinent of which Christendom had never heard, nor even
so much as had poetic vision,—unless, perchance, this
were the fabled Atlantis? Slowly, very slowly, exploration brought the facts to light; but even then men
were loath to receive the truth. When Vespucius brought
home authentic charts of new coasts in the southwest, thrust far out into the Atlantic, so that even mariners who strayed from their course to the Cape under
stress of storms from out the east might hit upon them,

Nunc vero & heę partes funt latius luftratæ/ &
alia quarta pars per Americũ Vefputium(vt in feʠ
quentibus audietur)inuenta ęft:quã non video cur
Ameʠ quis iure vetet ab Americo inuentore fagacis inge
rico niŋ viro Amerigen quafi Americi terram/fiue Ame
ricam dicendam:cum & Europa & Afia a mulieriʠ
bus fuá fortitá fint nomina.Eius fitũ & gentis moʠ
res ex bis binis Americi nauigationibus quę fequũ
tur liquide intelligi datur.

there was nothing for it but to deem this indeed a New
World. No such Asian coasts had ever been heard of
in that quarter of the globe. This southern world must,
no doubt, lie between Africa and the kingdoms of China.
But the northern continent had been found just where
the Asian coasts were said to lie. It was passing
hard to conceive it a mere wilderness, without civilization or any old order of settled life. Had Polo, after all,
been so deep a liar? Men would not so cheat their imaginations and balk their hopes of adventure. Un-
able to shake off their first infatuation, they went wistfully on, searching for kingdoms, for wonders, for some

native perfection, or else some store of accumulated bounty, until at last fancy was wholly baffled and rebuked by utmost discipline of total and disastrous failure. Not until a century had been wasted were confident adventurers sobered: the century of the Reformation and the Elizabethan literature. Then at last they accepted the task of winning America for what it was: a task of first settlement in a wilderness,—hard, unromantic, prodigious,—practicable only by strong-willed labor and dogged perseverance to the end.

While North America waited, South America prodigally afforded the spirit of the age what it craved. There men actually found what they had deemed Asia to contain. Here was, in fact, treasure-trove. The sea filled with mighty Spanish armaments, commanded by masters of conquest like Cortez; and the quaint and cloistered civilization of the New World trembled and fell to pieces under the rude blows of the Spanish soldiers. Then the sea filled again, this time with galleons deep-laden with the rich spoils of the romantic adventure. Whereupon daring English seamen like Hawkins and Drake turned buccaneers; and scant thought was given any longer to the forested wilds of North America. England and Spain faced each other on the seas. A few protestant sailors from the stout-hearted Devonshire ports undertook to make proud Spain smart for the iniquities wrought upon Englishmen by the Inquisition, while they lined their pockets, the while, out of Spanish bottoms. By the time the great Armada came, England had found her sea-legs. Spain recognized in the smartly handled craft which beat her clumsy galleons up the Channel the power that would some day drive her from the seas. Her hopes went to pieces with that

8

proud fleet, before English skill and prowess and pitiless sea-weather. It had been a century of preparation,
a century of vast schemes but half accomplished, of daring but not steadfast enterprise, of sudden sallies of

JOHN HAWKINS

audacious policy, but not of cautious plans or prudent
forecasts. The New World in the north still waited to
be used.

And yet much had in fact been accomplished towards
the future successful occupation of North America.
Some part of the real character of the new continent stood

sufficiently revealed. Early in the century Balboa had crossed the Isthmus and

> "Stared at the Pacific—and all his men
> Looked at each other with a wild surmise—
> Silent upon a peak in Darien."

SIR FRANCIS DRAKE

Magellan had found his way to the south, round about the coasts of South America, into the new ocean; and before the middle of the century Spanish vessels had beat their adventurous way along almost the entire Pacific length of both continents. By the time Drake set out on his famous first voyage round the world in 1577, the Spaniards had already established a trade route across the Pacific to India and the Spice Islands.

Their discoveries became very slowly known to the rest of the world; they had no mind to advertise what they found, and so invite rivalry. Each nation that coveted the new lands was left to find out for itself how they lay, with what coasts, upon what seas. It did at

"CROOK-BACKED" OX

last become generally known, however, that America was no part of Asia, but itself a separate continent, backed by an ocean greater even than the Atlantic. What was still hidden was the enormous extent of the New World. It had been found narrow enough from ocean to ocean at the Isthmus; and the voyagers along its farther coasts had not been expert to mark the real spread and trend of its outlines. They imagined it of no great bulk. Throughout the century every explorer who sought to penetrate its interior from the Atlantic

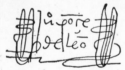

PONCE DE LEON

along any considerable watercourse confidently hoped to find, near the sources of the stream, similar passage down the western slopes of the continent to the great sea at the west. Adventurer after adventurer, moreover, pushed northward among the ice to find a northwest passage whereby to enter the Pacific.

All such mistakes only served to make the real character of the northern continent the more evident. Every discovery contributed to sober discoverers. That the interior was one vast wilderness, grown thick with tangled forests, blocked by mountains which stood old and untouched, or else stretching wide " through mighty plains and sandy heaths, smooth and wearisome, and bare of wood," with only " crook-backed oxen" for inhabitants, the Spaniards had abundantly discovered by many a costly adventure. In 1513, the year of Balboa's great discovery, and again in 1521, the gallant Ponce de Leon led an expedition into the beautiful peninsula which he named Florida, in search of a fabled spring whose waters, of " sweet savour and reflaire," it was said, " as it were of divers manner of spicery," would impart immortal youth to those who drank of them. But the wilderness baffled him, and he lost both his hope and his life in the enterprise.

In 1528 Pánfilo de Narvaez sought to take the land by storm, in true Spanish fashion, landing a force of three hundred men at Apalache Bay, with horses and trappings and stores, to march in quest of kingdoms and treasures. And march they did, thrusting their way through the forests and swamps very

SIGNATURE OF PÁNFILO DE NARVAEZ

manfully towards the vast unknown interior of the continent. Their ships, meanwhile, they sent away, to bring
still others to the enterprise, but with plans of rendez-
vous so vague and ill-conceived that they never beheld
them again. After three fruitless months spent with
keen suffering of want and disappointment in the wild
forests, where there was neither kingdom nor treasure,
they found themselves thrown back upon the coast
again, dismayed, and in search of their craft. Finding
that they must help themselves, they built such boats
as they could, and tried to pick their way by sea to the
westward. Caught in a rush of waters at the mouth of
the Mississippi, two of their five boats were overwhelmed,
and all who were in them were lost. The rest drifted on
till cast ashore far to the west. Four men, and four
only, of all the company survived to tell the story to the
world. After a marvellous and pitiful pilgrimage of
almost two thousand miles, full of every perilous and
strange adventure, they actually reached the Spanish
settlements on the Pacific, eight years after that gallant
landing at Apalache.

In 1539 Hernando de Soto repeated the folly. He
brought to the Bay of Espiritu Santo nine vessels, with
near six hundred men and more than two hundred horses.
Leaving a small part of his force with the fleet, he set out
with a great force for the interior of the continent. It
was childish folly; but it was gallantly done, with all
the audacity and hardness of purpose that distinguished Spanish conquest in that day. With contempt of
danger, meting out bitter scorn and cruelty to every
human foe, and facing even pitiless nature itself without blanching or turning back, proud and stubborn to
the last through every tormenting trial of the desper-

HERNANDO DE SOTO

ate march, they forced their way onward to the great waters of the Mississippi. From the mouth of that river, in boats of their own construction, some three hundred survivors reached Spanish posts on the Gulf.

15

But without their leader. De Soto had sickened and died as they beat up and down the wilderness which lay along the great stream of the Mississippi, whose inland courses he had discovered, and they had buried his body beneath its sluggish waters.

SIGNATURE OF CORONADO

Meanwhile a like expedition was wasting its strength in the wilds which stretched back from the Pacific. In 1540 Coronado, Spanish Governor of New Galicia, had led an army of three hundred Spaniards and eight hundred Indians northward from his Pacific province in search of seven fabled cities of "Cibola." These "cities" proved to be only humble pueblos such as those whose ruins still so curiously mark the river cliffs of Arizona and New Mexico. Having put out parties to explore the courses of the Colorado and the Rio Grande, only to find the stately cañons of the one, at the west, and the spreading valley of the other, at the south, without the notable peoples and provinces he looked for, he himself pressed doggedly onward for weary hundreds of miles, eastward and northeastward, to the far Missouri, to find at last nothing but vast deserts, without a trace of population or any slightest promise of treasure. It was a hard lesson thoroughly learned, bitten in by sufferings which corroded like deadly acids.

By such means was the real nature of the North American continent painfully disclosed, each maritime nation acting for itself. Spanish, English, and French seamen beat, time and again, up and down its coasts, viewing harbors, trying inlets, tracing the coast lines,

RUINS OF ARIZONA CLIFF-DWELLINGS

JACQUES CARTIER

carrying away rumors of the interior. The Spaniards explored and partially settled the coasts of the Gulf. In 1534-35 Jacques Cartier penetrated the St. Lawrence, in the name of his French master, as far as the present site of Montreal; and in 1541 planted a rude fort upon the heights of Quebec. In 1562--64 settlements of French Huguenots were effected in Florida, only to be destroyed, with savage ruthlessness, by the Spaniards, who in 1565 in their turn established St. Augustine, from which the French found it impossible permanently to dislodge them. In the opening years of the seventeenth century French colonies were planted on the St. Lawrence

OLD GATEWAY, ST. AUGUSTINE

at Montreal and Quebec, and in Acadia, in the region which was afterwards to be known as Nova Scotia. English settlements also were attempted. All signs combined to indicate the coming in of a new age of organized enterprise, when, with one accord, the nations which coveted the virgin continent should cease to

' fly to India for gold,
Ransack the ocean for Orient pearl,
And search all corners of the new-found world
For pleasant fruits and princely delicates,"

19

and should compete, instead, to build communities and erect states over sea, and so possess themselves of a vast treasure of their own making.

In the great enterprise of discovery and exploration Spain had held the first place throughout a century; but for the task of colonization the parts were to be differently cast. The century had witnessed many profound changes in European politics. In the year 1519 Charles V., King of Spain, Archduke of Austria, King of Naples and Sicily, heir of the House of Burgundy, and therefore lord of the Netherlands, had become also Emperor of Germany, and had begun to threaten all Europe with his greatness. But the vast circle of his realm had not held together. It was not a single power, but naturally diverse and disintegrate, and had speedily fallen asunder. In 1568 began that determined revolt of the Netherlands which was eventually to sap

ST. AUGUSTINE, FLORIDA, 1742

and destroy the Spanish power. By scattering her force too ambitiously, and staking her supremacy on

SIR MARTIN FROBISHER

too many issues, Spain began steadily to lose the great advantage she had held upon the continent. For England the end of Spain's power was marked by the destruction of the Armada, and the consequent dashing of all the ambitious schemes that had been put aboard the imposing fleet at Lisbon. There had meanwhile been reckonings between England and France also. Henry VIII. and Francis I. had kept restlessly at work to adjust the balance of European power to their own liking and advantage. Wars, brief and inconclusive, but ceaseless, swept Europe in every direction; and then radical changes set in, both national and international. In 1562 the great Huguenot civil wars broke out, to rage for more than twenty years; and France stained her annals with St. Bartholomew's day, 1572. In driving the Huguenots forth to England and America, she lost the flower of her industrial population. She thwarted her European enemies, nevertheless, and solidly compacted her national power. The German countries all the century through were torn and distracted by the struggle of the Reformation, and remained self-absorbed, forming the parties and defining the passions which were to bring upon them the terrible Thirty Years' War of the next century.

When the new century opened, France and England alone stood ready to compete for North America. And, for all France was as keen to seek her interest in the New World as in the Old, the signal advantage, as the event abundantly proved, was to lie with England in this new rivalry in the wilderness. The reason is now plain enough. England had obtained from the sixteenth century just the training she needed for winning America in the seventeenth, while France had unfitted herself for the race by the new life she had learned. England had become a commercial nation, quickened in every seaport by a bold spirit of individual enterprise that would dare anything for a success. The Tudor monarchs had, it is true, established a political absolutism; but they had, nevertheless, somehow deeply stirred individual initiative in their subjects in the process. In France, meanwhile, individual initiative had been stamped out, and the authority of church and state consolidated, to command and control every undertaking. France sent official fleets to America and established government posts; while England licensed trading companies, and left the colonists, who went to America in their own interest, to serve that interest by succeeding in their own way. The French colonies pined under careful official nursing; the English colonies throve under "a wise and salutary neglect." A churchly and official race could not win America. The task called for hard-headed business sense, patient, practical sagacity, and men free to follow their own interest by their own means.

The Reformation had performed a peculiar service for England. It had filled her, not with intense religious feeling, but with intense national feeling. It meant that England had thrown off all slavish political connection with Rome, and was to be henceforth national in her church as well as in her politics. It meant, too, that she was to have less church than formerly. When Henry VIII. destroyed the monasteries and appropriated their means and revenues, he secularized the government of England, and in part

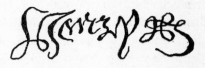

SIGNATURE OF HENRY VIII.

English society too, almost at a stroke. The wealth of the church went to make new men rich who had won the favor of the crown, and a new nobility of wealth began to eclipse the old nobility of blood. Such a change met the spirit of the age half-way. The quickened curiosity and nimble thought of the Renaissance had no courteous care as to what it exposed or upset. The discovery of new lands, moreover, stimulated all sorts of trade and sea-traffic. A general movement to learn and acquire new things had begun among masses of comfortable people who had never cared to disturb their minds before. The literature of the "spacious times of great Elizabeth" was the spontaneous speaking out, with unexampled freedom of heart, with unmatched boldness of fancy and amplitude of power, of the finer spirits of a nation excited by every new prospect of thought and enterprise. Fortunately the Tudor monarchs were stingy how they helped their subjects with money, even to defend their wealth and commerce against the foreigner. Henry VIII. interested himself in improved methods of ship-building; and when he had time to think of it he encouraged instruction in seamanship and navigation; but he built no navy. He even left the English coasts without adequate police, and suffered his subjects to defend themselves as best they might against the pirates who infested the seas not only, but came once and again to cut vessels out of port in England's own waters. Many public ships, it is true, had been built before the Armada came, and fine craft they were; but they were not enough. There was no real navy in the modern sense. The fleet which chased the Spaniards up the Channel was a volunteer fleet. Merchants had learned to defend their own cargoes. They built fighting craft of their own to keep their coasts and harbors free of pirates, and to carry their goods over sea.

They sought their fortunes as they pleased abroad, the crown annoying them with no inquiry to embarrass their search for Spanish treasure ships, or their trade in pirated linens and silks.

It was this self - helping race of Englishmen that

SPANISH GALLEON

matched their wits against French official schemes in America. We may see the stuff they were made of in the Devonshire seamen who first attempted the permanent settlement of the new continent. For a time all that was most characteristic of adventurous and sea-loving England was centred in Devonshire. Devonshire lies in the midst of that group of counties in the southwest of England in which Saxon mastery did least to destroy or drive out the old Celtic population.

SIR HUMPHREY GILBERT

There is, accordingly, a strong strain of Celtic blood among its people to this day; and the land suits with the strain. Its abrupt and broken headlands, its free

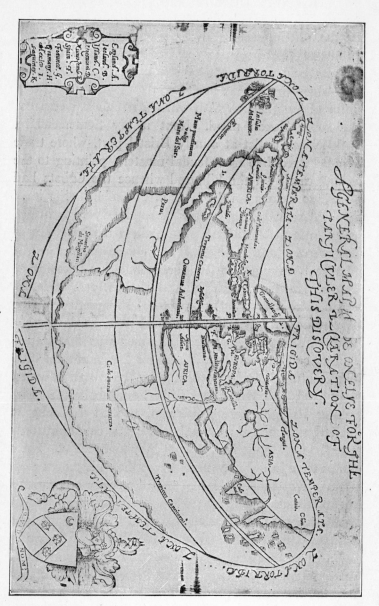

heaths and ancient growths of forests, its pure and genial air, freshened on either hand by the breath of the sea, its bold and sunny coasts, mark it a place made by nature to indulge that sense of mystery and that ardor of imagination with which the Celt has enriched the sober Saxon mind. Next it lay Somersetshire, with its sea outlet at sturdy Bristol port, where trade boasted itself free from feudal masters, pointing to the ruined castle on the hill, and whence the Cabots had sailed, so close upon the heels of Columbus. For itself Devonshire had the great harbor and roads of Plymouth, and innumerable fishing ports, where a whole race of venturesome and hardy fishermen were nurtured. All the great sea names of the Elizabethan age belong to it. Drake, Hawkins, Ralegh, and the Gilberts were all Devonshire men; and it was from Plymouth that the fleet went out which beat the great Armada on its way to shipwreck in the north. The men who first undertook to colonize the New World for England were bred to adventure, both by books and by the sea air in which they lived. Sir Humphrey Gilbert and his half-brother, Walter Ralegh, were gentlemen, trained to books at Oxford, and men of fortune besides, who could put forth into the world to look into what they had read of. Their books were full of travellers' tales; their neighbors were seamen who had met the Spaniard at close quarters on the high seas, and lightened him of his treasure. Wealth and adventure alike seemed to call them abroad into the new regions of the West. Ardently, and yet soberly too, with a steady business sagacity as well as with high, imaginative hope, they obtained license of the crown and led the way towards new ports and new homes in America. They did all with unstinted energy and de-

SIR WALTER RALEGH

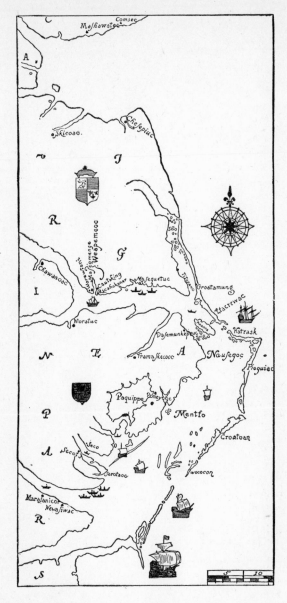

MAP OF ROANOKE ISLAND AND VICINITY BROUGHT AWAY BY THE
RALEGH COLONISTS

votion, embarking their fortunes in the venture. In 1583 Sir Humphrey Gilbert himself went out to Newfoundland, and lost his life seeking a harbor to the southward where to plant a colony. He had made his own quarters in the smallest vessel of his little fleet, and calmly "sat abaft with a book in his hand," even when the violent sea and the unknown coast threatened most sharply, cheering his companions the while with the stout-hearted assurance, "We are as near heaven by sea as by land." On Monday night, the 9th of September, about twelve o'clock, his lights went out and he found a haven he had not sought. The next year, 1584, Ralegh sent out two ships to take the southern course to America and find a coast suitable for settlement. They hit upon Roanoke Island. It was, their captains reported, an exceeding pleasant land, its people "most gentle, loving, and faithful, and such as live after the manner of the golden age." Within the next three years, therefore, until the coming of the Armada called his attention imperatively off from the business, Ralegh made two distinct efforts to establish a permanent colony on the island. But both attempts failed. The right temper and purpose had not come yet. The first colony contained men only, and these devoted themselves to exploration instead of to tillage and building. Ralegh and his agents alike were still dreaming of El Dorado. The second colony contained women and families; but they made small progress in learning to deal with the Indians, now no longer gentle and faithful; and they continued to rely on England for supplies, which did not come. When finally search was made for them they were not to be found. Their fate has remained a mystery to this day.

30

THE DISCOVERIE

OF THE LARGE, RICH AND BEVVTIFVL EMPIRE OF GVIANA, WITH

a relation of the Great and Golden Citie
of Manoa (which the spaniards call El
Dorado) And the prouinces of *Emeria*,
Arromaia, *Amapaia* and other Countries, with their riuers, ad-
ioyning

Performed in the yeare 1595. by Sir
W. Ralegh Knight, Captaine of her
Maiesties Guard, Lo. Warden
of the Stanneries, and her High-
nesse Lieutenant generall
of the Countie of
Cornewall.

Imprinted at London by Robert Robinson
1596.

TITLE-PAGE OF RALEGH'S "DISCOVERIE"

And so the century ended, with only a promise of what might some day be done. But, though the new continent still remained wild, strange, and inhospitable, the approaches to it at least were at length known. The Atlantic was cleared of its terrifying mystery, and the common sun shone everywhere upon it. Both the northern and the southern routes across it had become familiar to seafarers. The merchants of Southampton regularly sent ships upon the "commodious and gainful voyage to Brazil" so early as 1540; and Newfoundland had been a well-known fishing and trading post ever since 1504. In 1570 at least forty ships went annually from English ports to take part in the fisheries there; and in 1578 no fewer than a hundred and fifty were sent from France alone. Hundreds of crews were to be found in St. John's Harbor in the season, drying their catch and sunning their nets. Europe could not have been sure of fish on Fridays otherwise. The ocean ways were well known; the coast of North America was partly charted; its forests were no longer deemed the frontier barriers of kingdoms; the romantic age of mere adventure was past; and the more commonplace and sober age which succeeded was beginning to appreciate the unideal economic uses to which North America was to be put, if Europe was to use it at all. It only remained to find proper men and proper means for the purpose.

Note on the Authorities.—The general history of the discovery, exploration, and early settlement of the coasts of North America, before the English came, may best be read in the various chapters of the first two volumes of Winsor's *Narrative and Critical History of America* (where full lists of authorities are given), in the two volumes of Mr. John Fiske's *Discovery of America*, in the first volume of Mr. J. A. Doyle's *English Colonies in America*, and in the first volume of Bryant and Gay's excellent *Popular History of the United States*.   Mr. Francis Parkman has given a characteristically lucid, accurate, and engaging account of the French settlements in Florida and at the north in his *Pioneers of France in the New World*.

Those who wish to read of the early voyages and explorations at first hand, in the *contemporary accounts*, will find almost everything that they want in Richard Hakluyt's *Principal Navigations* (edited by Edmund Goldsmid.   Edinburgh, 16 vols., 1885–1890), in the invaluable *Publications* of the Hakluyt Society, and in the *Collections* of the Massachusetts Historical Society.

CHAPTER II

THE SWARMING OF THE ENGLISH

I. THE VIRGINIA COMPANY

IT was the end of the month of April, 1607, when three small vessels entered the lonely capes of the Chesapeake, bringing the little company who were to make the first permanent English settlement in America, at Jamestown, in Virginia. Elizabeth was dead. The masterful Tudor monarchs had passed from the stage, and James, the pedant king, was on the throne. The "Age of the Stuarts" had come, with its sinister policies and sure tokens of revolution. Men then living were to see Charles lie dead upon the scaffold at Whitehall. After that would come Cromwell; and then the second Charles, "restored," would go his giddy way through a demoralizing reign, and leave his sullen brother to face another revolution. It was to be an age of profound constitutional change, deeply significant for all the English world; and the colonies in America, notwithstanding their separate life and the breadth of the sea, were to feel all the deep stir of the fateful business. The revolution wrought at home might in crossing to them suffer a certain sea-change, but it would not lose its use or its strong flavor of principle.

The new settlers came in two small ships and a pinnace,

the *Goodspeed*, the *Sarah Constant*, and the *Discovery*, all of which belonged to the Muscovy Company, which usually sent its ships for trade much farther north, to Hudson's Bay and Davis Strait, or to bring cargoes

KING JAMES I.

from Greenland and the Cherry Islands. The little band of adventurers had gone aboard their craft at Blackwall, on the Thames, and had begun to drop down the river to put to sea on the next to the last day of December, 1606; but rough weather held them for weeks together in The Downs, and it was past the middle of February, 1607, before they got finally away. Their course fetched a wide compass round about by the Great Canaries and the West Indies in the south, and it was the end of April before they saw at last the strange coasts for which they were bound.

It was a lonely age in which to be four months upon the great sea, for "ships were rare," only "from time

THE GOODSPEED, SARAH CONSTANT, AND DISCOVERY AT THE CAPES OF THE DELAWARE

to time, like pilgrims, here and there crossing the waters." You were sure to see no sail anywhere as you went. And the land to which they came was as lonely as the sea, except for the savages who lurked within its forests. The three little merchantmen came none the less boldly in at the capes, however; and the tired men on board thought the shores of the vast bay within very beautiful, with their "fair meadows and goodly tall trees," and their "fresh waters running through the woods," better than any wine to men who for four months had drunk

"SHIPS WERE RARE'

from the stale casks on the ships. And yet the loneliness of those spreading coasts, forested to the very water, was enough to daunt even brave men.

They presently found a great "river on the south side, running into the main," and they chose a place on its banks for their settlement which was quite forty miles above the mouth of its stately stream; for they wished to be away from the open bay, where adventurous seamen of other nations, none too sure to be their friends, might at any time look in and find them. They named their river the James, and their settlement Jamestown, in honor of the king at home. Eighty years before there had been Spaniards upon that very spot. They had built houses there, and had planned to keep a lasting colony. There had been Spaniards in the West Indies these hundred years and more,—ever since the days of Columbus himself; and in 1526 Vasquez de Ayllon had led a great colony out of Santo Domingo to this very place, no fewer than five hundred persons, men and women, with priests to care for their souls and to preach the gospel to the savages. But discord, fever, and death had speedily put an end to the venture. The place had soon been abandoned. Scarcely one hundred and fifty of the luckless settlers survived to reach Santo Domingo again; and when the English put ashore there, where a tongue of low and fertile land was thrust invitingly into the stream, no trace remained to tell the tragic story. It was as still and bare and lonely a place as if no man else had ever looked upon it.

There were but a few more than a hundred men put ashore now from the English ships to try their hands at making a colony, and not a woman among them to make a home. They had been sent out by a mercantile company in London, as if to start a trading post, and not a community set up for its own sake, though there could be little trade for many a long day in that wilderness. Certain London merchants had united with certain west-country gentlemen and traders of Bristol, Exeter, and Plymouth in the formation of a joint-stock company for the purpose of setting up colonies in both "the north and south parts of Virginia"; and to this company royal letters patent had been issued on the 10th of April, 1606. The name "Virginia" had been given, in honor of Elizabeth, the Virgin Queen, to the mainland which Ralegh's first explorers found beyond Roanoke. So far as Englishmen were concerned, the name covered the greater part of the Atlantic coast of the continent. The patentees of the new company

"LIKE PILGRIMS, HERE AND THERE CROSSING THE WATERS"

were to attempt both a northern and a southern settlement, and, to serve their double purpose the better, were divided into two bodies. The London stockholders were to undertake the first colony, in some southern part of "Virginia," between the thirty-fourth and the forty-first degrees of north latitude; while the incorporators who were of Somerset and Devon were to undertake a

BOTH SIDES OF THE SEAL OF HIS MAJESTY'S COUNCIL OF VIRGINIA

second colony, to be conducted to some point farther north,—though all were to remain under the government of a single general council.

There were men of capital importance and quick energy among the London incorporators; and the enterprise they had taken in hand was not all novel. Several of them were members also of the East India Company, which had been formed seven years before, and of the "Russia or Muscovy Company," whose trade in far-away seas was a thing established and familiar.

DIVERS

voyages touching the discouerie of
America, *and the Ilands adiacent*
vnto the same, made first of all by our
*Englishmen, and afterward by the French-
men and Britons:*

And certaine notes of aduertisements for obserua-
tions, necessarie for such as shall heereafter
make the like attempt,

With two mappes annexed heereunto for the
plainer vnderstanding of the whole
matter.

**MVSEVM
BRITAN
NICVM**

Imprinted at Lon-

don for Thomas VVoodcocke,
dwelling in paules Church-yard,
at the signe of the blacke beare.

1582.

TITLE-PAGE OF HAKLUYT'S DIVERS VOYAGES

They were most of them men who had heard all there was to be told or read of the voyages and adventures by which America had become known in England; and some notable sailors were also of their number who had themselves seen the strange seas and unfamiliar coasts which others only read of. Richard Hakluyt, the genial and learned churchman, who loved every tale of daring and who knew more of the New World than any other man in

RICHARD HAKLUYT

the kingdom, was their associate in the new company. Captain Newport, to whom they intrusted the command of their little fleet, borrowed from the Muscovy Company, had already been twice to America: a clear-eyed man hardly turned of forty, and likely to understand what he saw. Bartholomew Gosnold, whom they commissioned captain of the *Goodspeed*, had himself discovered the short route to America by way of the Azores, and went now permanently to cast in his lot with the colonists. There were capacity and experience and audacity and steadfastness enough embarked in the service of the Virginia Company, it must have seemed, to make it sure of its success.

And yet nobody very well understood what this new business of establishing colonies was to be like, for all that; and the colonists whom these capable London gentlemen sent over with Captain Newport were a sorry lot, it turned out, with whom to attempt an enterprise which should need for its execution every manly quality of courage and steadfastness and industry. Prosperous and steady men who were succeeding at home were not likely to be willing to go to America, of which they knew nothing except that it was full of savages, and that

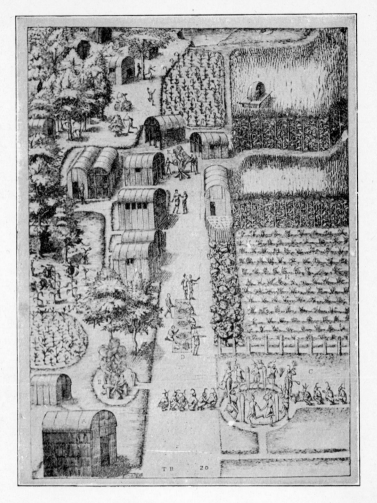

INDIAN VILLAGE OF SECOTAN

Ralegh's colonists had been lost there, never to be found again. Only men hopelessly out of work or out of sorts, and reckless men, young and fond of adventure, were likely to think the prospect inviting, or the novel risk worth taking, to better their fortunes, or to get the monotony out of their lives.

It happened that England was full of idle men, because her life was changing. The very quickening and expansion of commerce and of adventure in trade and conquest which had changed all the age and the aspect of the world itself since the first crossing of the Atlantic had given England a new place in the geography of the planet, and was radically altering men's lives and occupations and ambitions there. New trades and industries were springing up, and the towns were reaping the benefits of a diversified commerce. But the people of the rural districts had fallen upon evil days. Land, like everything else, had become a sort of commodity as trade gained its mastery. The old tenures, under which small holders had so long lived unmolested, were breaking up. The city merchants bought estates for their pleasure, and wanted no tenants. The older landowners got rid of small farmers as fast as they could, in order to turn their lands into pasture for the sheep whose wool was so much in demand by the merchants and the manufacturers. They even enclosed and appropriated for the same purpose commons which had time out of mind been free to all, and swept hamlets away to make the more room for their flocks. The demand for agricultural labor sadly slackened. "Your sheep, that were wont to be so meek and tame," cried Sir Thomas More, in his anger and pity to see such things done, "are now become so great devourers and so wild that they eat up and swallow down the very men themselves. They consume, devour, and destroy whole fields, houses, and cities." Town and countryside alike filled with men out of work, who "prowled

44

about as idle beggars or continued as stark thieves till the gallows did eat them''; and unguarded wayfarers were robbed upon the highways by desperate men who could find no other way to obtain subsistence. James's craven eagerness for peace had put an end to the wars with which Elizabeth's day had resounded, and London was full of idle soldiers, mustered out of service. Younger sons and decayed and ruined gentlemen seemed to abound more than ever.

It was men out of work or unfit for it who chose to go to America; and not men of the country-sides so much as discredited idlers and would-be adventurers of the towns. More than one-half of the company Captain Newport conducted to James River called themselves "gentlemen,"—were men, that is, of good blood enough, but no patrimony, no occupation, no steady habit, who were looking for adventure or some happy change of fortune in a new land, of which they knew nothing at all. Very few, indeed, of the rest were husbandmen or carpenters or trained laborers of any sort. There was only one mason, only one blacksmith, in all the hundred and twenty. Only two were bricklayers, only six carpenters; while thirty-five were gentlemen, and most knew not what to call themselves. The things it was most necessary to do when at last the landing had been made at Jamestown,—the planting of crops, the building of houses, the dull labor of felling trees and making a beginning in a wilderness,—were the very things which the men the Virginia Company had sent over knew least about, and had the least inclination to learn. They expected the company to send them supplies out of England, and gave little thought to what they were to do for themselves. When Captain Newport's ships put to sea again and left them, they were at their wits' ends to know how to maintain themselves.

It would have gone desperately with them had there not been one or two men of masterful temper and governing talents among them. Captain Newport came again with supplies in the winter; and still another ship followed him the next spring. And, besides supplies, the two ships brought a hundred and twenty new settlers between them. But among the new-comers there were shiftless "gentlemen" in the usual proportion; and there came with them a jeweller, two goldsmiths, two refiners, and a perfumer,—as if there would be need of such people! Such additions to the settlement only made it so much the harder to develop or even maintain it; and the few men who could rule stood out like masters among the inefficient idlers of whom the incorporators in London had thought to make pioneers.

There was one among them, Captain John Smith, to whom, in large part at any rate, they owed their salvation from utter helplessness and starvation. Captain Smith had a gift for narrative which his fellow-adventurers did not have, and has set his own achievements down in notable books whose direct and rugged ways of speech, downright temper of action, and air of hardihood bespeak the man himself. He was not yet thirty years of age when he began to play his part there in Virginia; he was exasperatingly sure of himself; older men found his pretensions wellnigh unbearable. But it was certain he had seen more of the world and of adventure than any other man of the company. He had known and had come to conclusions with men of many races and of every kidney, as

A TRVE RE
lation of ſuch occur-

rences and accidents of noateas
hath hapned in Virginia ſince the firſt
planting of that Collony, which is now
reſident in the South part thereof, till
the laſt returne from
thence.

Written by Captaine Smith *one of the ſaid Collony, to a
woiſhipfull friend of his in England.*

LONDON
Printed for *Iohn Tappe*, and are to be ſolde at the Grey-
hound in Paules-Church-yard, by *W. W.*
1608

TITLE-PAGE OF CAPTAIN JOHN SMITH'S "TRUE RELATION"

he had cast about the world, a soldier of fortune; and he knew how they were to be governed, as he presently demonstrated. He rang like brass without, no doubt, but had a quality of gold within. He was a partisan of his own way of making a colony, and it may be colored the narratives he wrote to be seen at home; but he was no sluggard at work, and knew how to take the burdens of tasks which no one else would attempt. He at least found ways of getting food from the Indians, and of making interest with their chiefs. Though he took authority when it was not given him, he made the lazy, "humoursome, and tuftaffety sparks" of the settlement work, upon penalty of being set across the broad river to shift for themselves or starve; prevented would-be deserters from running away with the boats; explored the neighboring coasts and river-courses,—for two years and a half played his part very capably and very manfully in keeping the struggling settlement alive, when the majority of his comrades would have been glad to abandon it. He compelled no man to do what he did not willingly do himself. "Gentlemen," under the spur of his example and command, learned to make a pleasant pastime of labor in the forest,—so that "thirty or forty of such voluntary gentlemen," as Master Anas Todkill said, "would do more in a day than one hundred of the rest that must be prest to it by compulsion,"—though doubtless "twenty good workmen would have been better than them all." No doubt there were others who seconded Captain Smith in the maintenance of order and of hope, and who worked as he did to take some hold upon the wilderness for their principals at home; but upon him fell the chief burden of the task, because he could carry it and prevail.

When at last, in the autumn of 1609, he was obliged to take ship for England, dangerously wounded by an explosion of gunpowder, it looked as if the worst were over at Jamestown. The company at home had been very busy getting colonists, and had sent them over in goodly numbers. There were about five hundred

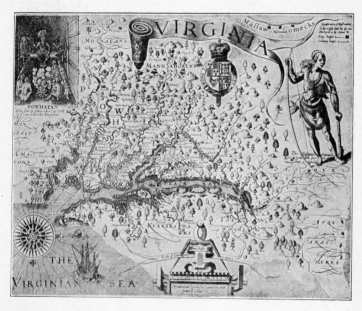

CAPTAIN JOHN SMITH'S MAP OF VIRGINIA, 1612

persons at the settlement when Captain Smith left,— a few women among them, making it look at last as if the lonely place were to see homes established; and fifty or sixty simple houses had been put up. But numbers, it turned out, did not improve the living. Too many of the new-comers were "unruly gallants, packed thither by their friends to escape ill destinies" at home; and those whom they joined at their landing still did not

I.—4

know how to support themselves in the wilderness, or
how to keep themselves safe against the fevers which
lurked within the damp forests by the river. Added
numbers made them a little more helpless than before;
and the six months which immediately followed Captain Smith's departure brought upon them a desperate
"starving time," which no man who survived it ever
forgot. There were few to work where every one was
ill and in want. They tore their rude houses down
for firewood before the winter was over; do what they
could, only sixty of them lived to see the spring again,
and a gleam as of madness played in the eyes of those
who survived those days of desolation. One came and
cast his Bible into the fire, crying out that there was no
God. It was resolved at last, when they could, to abandon the desolate and hopeless place, and the forlorn little
band were actually on their way down the river, meaning to seek food and shelter among the fishermen in
Newfoundland, when Lord Delaware met them at its
very mouth with fresh colonists and supplies sent by
the company to their relief.

The radical difficulty was, not that the company did
not do its part to sustain the colony, but that it could
get few colonists of the proper sort, and was trying to
do an impossible thing. The settlers sent out had no
hopes or prospects of their own, as the company managed the business then. They were simply its servants,
fed out of a common store, and settled upon land which
belonged to no one but was used for all alike. No man
would work well or with quick intelligence if he could
not work at all for himself, but must always be working
for the company. First-rate men would not consent
to be the company's drudges. And what could the

TITLE-PAGE OF CAPTAIN JOHN SMITH'S "GENERALL HISTORIE"

company get out of the wilderness in return for its out-
lay by the work of such men as it could induce to go to
Virginia upon such terms? A few cargoes of timber,
a few new varieties of medicinal herbs found in the forests, could not make such expenditure worth while.
Captain Newport, after his second voyage out, had
gone back to England with his hold full of glistening
earth, which he supposed to contain gold; but it contained nothing of the kind. It was only shining sand.

Lord Delaware, though a little slow and stiff and
fond of wearing fine apparel and going about attended
by officers and halberd-bearers, which seemed fantastic
enough there in the shadow of the untouched forests
of that wilderness, was a wise and capable man, and
no doubt saved the colony by coming out, that hopeless spring of 1610, as Governor and Captain General
for the company. But it needed a radically new policy
to give real life to such an enterprise; and that it did not
get till Sir Thomas Dale came the next year (1611), after Lord Delaware had gone home stricken with a fever.
The new policy it needed was one which should give it
expansion and a natural vitality of its own. It was
necessary that new towns should be built upon the river
which should not be, like Jamestown, mere stations
where men worked at tasks for the company, but veritable communities in which men should be allowed to
have land of their own, and should be given leave to
work for themselves as well as for the incorporators in
London. For five years (1611–1616) Sir Thomas Dale
and Sir Thomas Gates pushed this new policy forward;
and it was their new and better way of doing things
that really made and established Virginia. "Henri-
cus," "Hampton," "New Bermuda," and other new

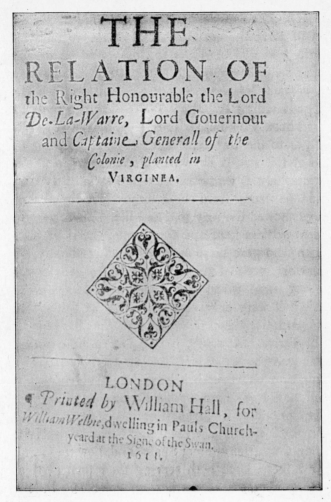

THE

RELATION OF

the Right Honourable the Lord
De-La-Warre, Lord Gouernour
and *Captaine* Generall of the
Colonie, *planted in*
VIRGINEA.

LONDON
Printed *by* William Hall, for
William Welbie, dwelling in Pauls Church-
yeard at the Signe of the Swan.
1611.

TITLE-PAGE OF LORD DELAWARE'S "RELATION"

settlements like them, were added to Jamestown, each
with its fort and its stockade, its military commander
and discipline, and each with its group of virtually independent landowners, free to work for themselves.

Most of the colonists, it is true, were still held at James-town to serve the company, and driven to their work, as little better than slaves, by their new task-masters. Gates and Dale came with authority to rule by martial law, without let or mercy, and colonists of the poorer sort got nothing but blows and rations for their bitter toil. Those who mutinied or ran away were put to death or to the torture, if need were, to keep the discipline of toil and order which the company's treasurer and merchant adventurers were now steadfastly minded should be wrung from the colony. But the new plantations showed the way to a new life. There were independent settlers here and there upon the river, as well as men who were mere servants of the company. The better sort, even of the men whom the company had sent out, were given their patches of land and their time,—if it were only one month out of the twelve,—to do work for themselves, in order that the new plans might thrive. A strong root as of a little commonwealth was planted at last.

Dale and Gates both belonged to that capable race which had been bred under Elizabeth, willing to be soldiers or sailors by turns, if only they could be always in the thick of action. They had both been soldiers in the Low Countries against Spain, and, now that fighting flagged there, were both serving their turn at this interesting business of setting up colonies. Dale was the more capable and masterful of the two: a terror to men who would not work or were slow to obey; a leader after their own hearts for men who meant to do their tasks and succeed,—and his stay in Virginia was, fortunately, longer by three years than Gates's. He was but Gates's deputy so long as Gates was in Virginia

(1611–1613); but he was master when Gates was gone, —prevailed even when Gates was there,—and it was his rough and soldierly energy which made the little group of "plantations" at least ready to last and to expand into a lusty piece of England over sea. When he had finished his five years' work, the colony, though small and primitive still, was yet strong and spirited enough to survive being despoiled by an adventurer. For a year after Dale quit the colony it was left under the government of Captain George Yeardley, the commandant of one of the new settlements. But in 1617 Samuel Argall came out to take his place, and proved himself no lover of

the people he had come to govern, but a man chiefly bent upon serving his own fortunes. He was of gentle blood, but had too long followed the sea in those disordered times, as little better than a freebooter, to relish law or justice overmuch; and it was excellent proof that the colony had grown strong and able to take care of itself that it endured for full two years his tyrannous and selfish exactions (1617–1619), and yet was ready at the end of them to assume a sort of independence, under a new form of government which gave it the right to make its own laws.

In 1619 Captain Yeardley, now become Sir George, returned out of England commissioned to take Argall's place and govern the plantations under a new and better charter. He was to call together an assembly of representatives from the several plantations, and that assembly, sitting with the governor's council, was to have the full right to make laws for the colony, subject always to the approval of the court of the company sitting in London. Here was a very radical change. The colony was to be no longer the mere mercantile venture of a trading company controlled by its stockholders. It was to be a little state, governed by its people. The fact was that a notable change had come over the company at home. Until now it had been managed by men who were mere merchants, not statesmen: by men who cared very little about anything but the profits some time to be got out of the colony,—the sooner the better. Now men of another sort were in control; the chief among them Sir Edwin Sandys, a man who loved liberty, had a statesman's knowledge how it was to be set up and maintained, and wished to see the settlement thrive for its own sake, and the noble Earl of Southampton, whom Shakespeare loved. It was upon the initiative of these men that Sir George Yeardley had been sent out to give the colony self-government.

Here, under the quiet forms of a mere administrative change in the management of the colony, was a veritable revolution wrought. Sir George brought with him a document, bearing date 13 November, 1618, which Virginians were always thenceforth to look back to as to their Great Charter of rights and liberties,—a document which made of their colony a little commonwealth. It was drawn in the spirit of the men for whom Sandys spoke. Five years ago Sir Edwin had stood in his place in the Commons and maintained in the face of all present "that the origin of every monarchy lay in election; that the people gave its consent to the king's authority upon an express understanding that there were

56

To my honourable frend Sr George yearley
knight gouernor of virginia.

Sr I comend vnto yow my good faborr and trew Loue
begyninge Richard ho of Sr villiam Throkmorton an
m: George Thorpe (who is of Sr... Soune(?))...
... George yearly apoynted...
...

London 3. August
1619

your assured loveinge frind
Thomas Canninge

certain reciprocal conditions which neither the king nor the people might violate with impunity; and that a king who pretended to rule by any other title, such as that of conquest, might be dethroned whenever there was force sufficient to overthrow him "; and here was now a constitution for Virginia drawn in like spirit. No wonder the King had cried, " Choose the devil, if you will, but not Sir Edwin Sandys," when he heard that the Virginia Company had a mind to make this too free-thinking friend of Hooker and Selden its chief and treasurer, and deemed it revolutionized and made an instrument of sedition against him when it chose Sir Edwin notwithstanding.

The new Virginian assembly met in the chancel of the church at Jamestown, on the 30th of July, 1619. We look back with some emotion upon it, as to the first representative assembly in America,—as to the beginning of liberty and self-government in the English colonies; but the colonists themselves seem to have taken it very quietly, as if they had expected it and looked upon it almost as a matter of course in the circumstances. Its sessions were as brief, as businesslike, and as much without ado as if they were already an established part of the custom of the colony. Certain necessary enactments were adopted touching trade with the Indians, the use of tobacco as currency, the salaries and authority of clergymen, and various other matters in which special regulations for Virginia seemed called for; but for the rest it was taken for granted that the common law of England was in force there, as in every other place where there were Englishmen; and within six days of its coming together the little assembly was ready to adjourn. The quiet and ready capacity with which the

FIRST VIRGINIA ASSEMBLY—GOVERNOR YEARDLEY PRESIDING

colonists accepted this radical change in the method of their life and government afforded the best proof that they were fit for the responsibilities it involved.

The company, under its new leaders, was a little too eager to help the colony to prosper. Settlers were hurried over much faster than they could be provided for. During the three years 1619–1621 quite three thousand five hundred came pouring in, men, women, and children, fleet after fleet of the company's ships appearing in the river to put their mixed hosts of inexperienced people ashore. And yet at the end of the three years there were but twelve hundred settlers, all told, in the colony. Cleared land and means of immediate subsistence could not be found upon short notice for so many. Hundreds succumbed to the dangerous fevers and sudden distempers drawn out of the damp forests by the summer sun or the first chill of the autumn nights. A sore process of "seasoning" tried out the river settlements every year, and only a few could endure it. It was reckoned inevitable that hundreds of new-comers should die. Many saw how things stood and went back to England again. But those who remained and survived prospered well; and the settlements grew, after all, as fast as it was safe for them to grow.

The terms under which land was granted to settlers became more and more liberal as things settled to an established way of life. Even Dale had not relieved the tenants of his day from the duty of working part of their time for the company; and the colony had been conducted, until Sir George Yeardley came, like a joint-stock enterprise in which only stockholders might expect private profit. But under the changed conditions which followed Sir George's coming virtually inde-

LANDING OF NEGROES AT JAMESTOWN FROM A DUTCH MAN-OF-WAR, 1619

pendent landholding became possible on very easy terms; and, what was quite as good, the company no longer insisted that everything bought or sold should pass through the hands of their factor, as the only middle-man, so that the profits of all trade might fall to them. It turned out to be a very important thing that Mr. John Rolfe, one of the colonists, had in 1612 introduced

SIGNATURE OF SIR THOMAS DALE

the cultivation of tobacco; for tobacco grew amazingly well and of exceeding good quality in Virginia, and proved a most profitable crop. By 1620 forty thousand pounds of the delectable herb were exported from the colony in a single year, and everybody who could was planting tobacco instead of grain. Its leaves even became the currency of the plantations, coin being very scarce. "The people of the South-parts of Virginia," it was reported, "say that God in the creation did first make a woman, then a man, thirdly great maize or Indian wheat, and fourthly, Tobacco."

In 1619, the year Sir George Yeardley came to set up an assembly, another very notable thing happened. A Dutch man-of-war came into the river and sold twenty negroes to the colonists as slaves. A handful of slaves made no great difference at first; they were so few as scarcely to affect the life of the colony, and it was to be many a long day before their number was much added to. But their coming was the beginning of a great change which was slowly, very slowly, to alter the whole face of society in the settlements.

By 1622 it seemed as if the chief difficulties of settlement were safely passed and the plantations secure of their growth and permanence. But in the very moment of assurance a great calamity came upon them, sudden, overwhelming, like a bolt out of a clear sky. On the same day and at the same hour (22d of March, 1622) the Indians fell upon every settlement from the

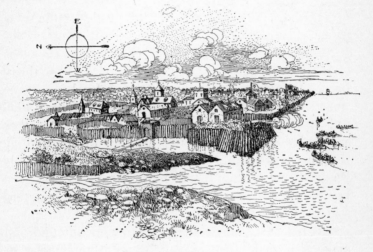

JAMESTOWN IN 1622

falls of the river to the bay, all the tribes of all the region round mustering in concert to strike a single exterminating blow. The colonists had suffered themselves to be deceived by the submissive friendliness of their savage neighbors, and had grown strangely heedless of danger from them. For years they had traded with them, mingled with them, admitted them freely to their homes, taught them the expert use of fire-arms, made servants and even confidants of them, without caution or reserve, deeming them an inferior race who

had accepted the white men as masters. But the old Powhatan, a real friend of the English, who had been ruler
among the redmen ever since the landing at Jamestown,
was dead. Opecanchanough, their subtle and implacable enemy, had succeeded him. For four years the
wily savage had been drawing the tribes together for a
decisive treachery; and the dreadful secret had all the
while been kept safe behind the steady eyes of every
Indian who entered the settlements. Only at the last
moment did one or two faithful native servants warn
their masters of the fearful peril; and then it was too
late to do more than put a few households on their
guard. Before the sun went down that fatal day three
hundred and forty-seven men, women, and children lay
dead in the desolate settlements. Only because the
Indians feared the white man with an overmastering
dread, and drew back dismayed wherever a firm stand
was made against them, if only by a single settler
barred within his house, did the terrible slaughter stop
short of sheer annihilation. No place escaped the car-
nage. But the colony, though stunned, was not killed.
The Indians' courage had not held out to finish the
bloody work. There was henceforth an endless reckoning in store for them,—no longer any friendship vouch-
safed or any consideration. Steadily, relentlessly, and
by a masterful advance from settlement to settlement
which they could in no wise withstand, they were
pushed back into the forests. The very year which
followed the massacre found nearly two thousand white
men still in the scattered villages and plantations of
the indomitable English, and their quiet way of growth
had been resumed.

But the great company which had founded the settlements and seen them safely through their first struggles for life and maintenance was not to be suffered to live. The King did not relish the politics and suspected the loyalty of the gentlemen who were in charge of its affairs. They were of the party which opposed him in Parliament. He had dismissed his Parliament and

GRAVE OF POWHATAN

meant to rule without it; but this great company, with names upon its rolls which were among the chief of London not only but of the kingdom itself, held meetings every quarter under his very eyes which were like another parliament; which brought his enemies very near him, and held the attention of the town. Those who wished his favor or the ruin of Sandys and Southampton told him that they used their conferences to plot sedition against him, and the councils of the company to keep a constitutional opposition together; and he determined to be rid of them. Every mismanaged or ill-judged affair with which the company was chargeable was magnified and made the most of, and, despite a very gallant fight in the law courts to save it, its

ALL THAT IS LEFT OF JAMESTOWN

charter was taken away, and the government of the colony transferred to the hands of the King and his ministers. It made little practical difference to the colonists. They kept their assembly, and could live as comfortably under a governor sent them by the King as under a governor sent them by the company. The course of affairs in Virginia was not disturbed. But a great company was destroyed, and the public-spirited men who had given it its best life and the

66

colony its first taste of self-pleasing liberty were deeply wronged.

Authorities on the history of Virginia during the seventeenth century. Excellent general narratives of the founding and early development of Virginia are to be found in the first volume of Mr. John A. Doyle's *English Colonies in America* and in Mr. John Fiske's *Old Virginia and Her Neighbours.* Charles Campbell's *History of the Colony and Ancient Dominion of Virginia* is the standard history of the colony; John Burk's *History of Virginia* is the most solid and extensive of the older accounts; and Robert R. Howison's *History of Virginia* has the dignity of resting upon careful research. William Stith's *History of the First Discovery and Settlement of Virginia* brings the narrative down only to 1624, but is compact of the most interesting matter, and is a significant example of the scholarship of the middle of the eighteenth century in Virginia. Mr. Stith was President of William and Mary College. The Rev. Hugh Jones's *Present State of Virginia* was published in 1724, and is an excellent early authority. Miss Ann Maury's *Memoirs of a Huguenot Family* contains the authentic records and letters of three generations of a family driven from France to Virginia by the revocation of the Edict of Nantes, and affords a very intimate picture of the life of more than a century. The Rev. E. D. Neill, in his *History of the Virginia Company of London,* his *Virginia Vetusta,* and his *Virginia Carolorum,* has brought together a vast deal of scattered information out of which very direct impressions may be got of the life and history of the colony. Bishop Meade, in his *Old Churches and Families of Virginia,* has brought together an extraordinary mass of authentic details, most of which relate to the eighteenth, but many of which belong to the seventeenth century.

The *original sources* of Virginian history are to be found in Captain John Smith's *True Relation of Such Occurences as Have Happened in Virginia,* published in 1608, and *Generall Historie,* published in 1624, both of which many modern readers are inclined to take with a grain of salt; in the *Collections* of the Virginia Historical Society (which, among many other important things, contain the Proceedings of the Virginia Company from 1619 to 1624); in W. W. Hening's invaluable and remarkable collection of the *Statutes at Large* of Virginia, which begins with the acts of the first assembly, in 1619, and is brought down, with scarcely an omission, to the end of the eighteenth century; in Sainsbury's *Calendar of* [English] *State Papers, Colonial,* I. and V.; in the two volumes of Mr. Alexander Brown's *Genesis of the United States,* which is a notable mine of material; in Peter Force's *Tracts and Other Papers Relating to the Colonies in North America;* in the *Collections* of the Massachusetts Historical Society; in the notable collection of papers gathered under the title *Archaeologia Americana;* in the *Virginia Historical Register:* in the *Virginia Magazine of History and Biography;* and in the *Southern Literary Messenger.*

MEANWHILE other colonies were being successfully planted in the north. On the great river St. Lawrence, which doughty Jacques Cartier had explored quite seventy years before, the French had set up trading-posts at Montreal and Quebec. They had established, besides, a struggling settlement or two nearer the mouth of the river; and to the southward, within the Bay of Fundy. A little colony of Englishmen had begun to make homes for themselves in Newfoundland. Dutch traders were established on the Hudson. A company of English dissenters were building a New Plymouth within Cape Cod, and little groups of English adventurers were trying to secure a foothold upon the southern shores of the wide Bay of Massachusetts. Nowhere except in Virginia had more than a beginning been made; but the settlement of the continent seemed at last to have been begun in earnest; and the future looked interesting enough with the French, the Dutch, and the English all entered as active competitors in the race for possession.

The Dutch were likely to be harder rivals to beat than the French. Their little, compact home states in the Netherlands were, it is true, scarcely one-fourth as big as England, but they teemed with a thrifty people almost as numerous as the English themselves, and their chief power was upon the sea. With them, at home, the very land itself was one-half sea. They had been bred fishermen and mariners time out of mind; and of late, because the Spaniard provoked them to it, they had put great fleets on the high seas and had made conquests at the ends of the earth.

At first they had not thought of conquest. They had simply made themselves, with their stout craft and seasoned tars, the ocean carriers for Europe,—because the Portuguese, who had captured rich lands and set

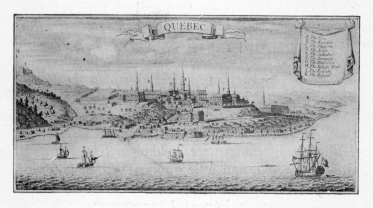

VIEW OF QUEBEC ABOUT 1732

up a great trade all the way from the Persian Gulf to Japan, did not trouble themselves to bring their cargoes beyond their own port of Lisbon, and because the Spaniards brought their treasures out of South America no farther than Seville, and some one was needed to carry what they would sell to the merchants and princes of the rest of Europe. No doubt the Dutch would have been content to be only traders and carriers, had Spain but let them alone. But Spain, in her folly, undertook to force the Dutch to be Roman Catholics; and they, being stout Protestants and stubborn

A
DESCRIPTION
of *New England:*

OR

THE OBSERVATIONS, AND
difcoueries, of Captain *Iohn Smith* (Admirall
of that Country) in the North of *America*, in the year
of our Lord 1614 : *with the fucceffe of fixe Ships,
that went the next yeare* 1615 ; *and the*
accidents befell him among the
French men of warre:

With the proofe of the prefent benefit this
Countrey affoords: whither this prefent yeare,
*1616, eight voluntary Ships are gone
to make further tryall.*

At LONDON
Printed by *Humfrey Lownes,* for *Robert Clerke ;* and
are to be fould at his houfe called the Lodge,
in Chancery lane, ouer againft Lin-
colnes Inne. 1616.

TITLE-PAGE OF JOHN SMITH'S "DESCRIPTION OF NEW ENGLAND"

men, resisted after a fashion that in the end set the whole power of rich Spain at naught. The war began in 1568; all Europe was stirred by it; and when, forty-one years later, the Spaniard, quite out of breath, agreed to a truce, the world had changed. Holland had become a great sea-power; had driven the Portuguese from the Orient, taking their trade and their colonies; was sinking imperial fleets upon the very coasts of Spain herself, and sweeping Spanish treasure by the ship's cargo into her own coffers. She was beforehand even with England in making herself mistress of the seas, and had turned to this new task of taking possession of America with confidence and audacity.

The Dutch combined conquest with trade, as England did, and it was a Dutch East India Company of merchants which drove the Portuguese from their possessions in the East, as it was an English East India Company of merchants which afterwards conquered India for England. And when their East India Company had made itself powerful and famous by its conquests and adventures, the Dutch formed a West India Company also, to trade and take what it could upon the western coasts of Africa, upon both coasts of South America, and among the southern islands of the Atlantic. It had, as Mr. Motley has said, a roving commission to trade and fight and govern for twenty-four years; and it incidentally undertook to establish Dutch settlements on the Hudson and the Delaware. Henry Hudson, an English sailor in the service of the Dutch East India Company, had, in the year 1609, discovered the great river which was to bear his name,—the very year the baffled Spanish agreed to a truce with the redoubtable states of the Netherlands. He had also entered the great bay and stream of the Delaware. The Dutch had promptly named the Hudson the "Great North River," the Delaware the "South River," and all the rich country which lay about and between them "New Netherland"; meaning from the first to keep and occupy what their seamen had found.

There had been a New Netherland Company, formed

EARLIEST VIEW OF NEW AMSTERDAM

in 1614, before there was a West India Company. Its charter had given it commercial control of all the coast country of America from forty to forty-five degrees north latitude, a region which the Dutch described as lying "between New France [on the north] and Virginia." This was at the very heart of the country which James of England had granted to the Virginia Company; but the Dutch knew little of that, and would very likely have thought as little had they known more. It was the profitable fur trade with the Indians

73

of the Great North River that had first attracted them. Individual adventurers among them had built a small "fort" or trading post far up the river in the heart of the wilderness, as well as a little group of huts on the seaward point of Manhattan Island in the bay, and had been trafficking there with the willing natives for quite four years before they formed their New Netherland Company.

It was the New Netherland Company that grew into the greater West India Company, whose principal business it was to be to wrest what it could from the Portuguese and the Spanish in the south, but which was also to keep an eye all the while on the North and South rivers, where the New Netherland Company had put its trading posts. It was 1623 before the great company found time amid its other business to carry out any systematic plans of settlement in North America; but by 1625 there were already two hundred colonists on the lands they claimed: some up the great stream of the North River at the little post which they called Fort Orange, some within the South River at "Fort Nassau," some on Manhattan Island, a few on Long Island,—even a little group of families as far away as the "Fresh River," which the English were to call the Connecticut. It remained to be seen how they would fare scattered there in the wilderness; but there they were, a very hard people to discourage, by the time Virginia was fairly established in its own scattered settlements on the James, and the rights of the great Virginia Company taken into the hands of the King,—and there they meant to stay.

Meanwhile there had come out from Holland itself a band of exiled English settlers, to be their neighbors

and rivals at the north, and so put them between two growing English colonies,—not "between New France and Virginia," as their first charter had said, but between New England and Virginia. The new-comers were exchanging a temporary exile in Holland for a permanent exile in America, and effected their settlement within the sheltering arm of Cape Cod. Englishmen had begun to muster many thousands strong in Holland within a generation, and the two countries had been drawn very near to each other. Long before the war began which brought Spain and the Netherlands to a grapple, hundreds of English merchants had established themselves in the Dutch seaports; and young Englishmen were beginning, even before dissenters were shut out from Oxford and Cambridge, to resort in influential numbers to the Dutch universities. When the Low Countries grappled with Spain, English volunteers crowded into their armies. The troops Elizabeth sent over after 1585 found the Dutch ranks already full of their countrymen. English churchmen, too, for whom the policy of the Establishment proved too rigorous under the imperious Tudor queens, had learned to seek in Holland the freedom of worship denied them at home. At the same time refugees from the ravage and slaughter of Alva's armies poured across the sea from the lower Netherlands into England, and the two countries seemed to be exchanging populations. Tradesmen, weavers, mechanics, farmers, fled terror-stricken into the eastern and southern counties of England, often braving the sea in open boats when danger pressed most desperately. Their coveted skill and industry, which English statesmen knew how to value, their foreign birth and humble rank in life, which seemed to depress them below the level of political influence, gained for them an indulgence in theological error and separate worship which was denied to Englishmen themselves, and presently the English towns in the east and south teemed with thousands of Dutch artisans, who were suffered to be Anabaptists, Lutherans,—what they would, so long as they taught England the industries and handicrafts which were to make her rich.

The little company of Englishmen who, in 1620, ex-

THE MAYFLOWER IN PLYMOUTH HARBOR

changed Holland for America were not soldiers and traders like the men who had led and established the colony at Jamestown, but members, most of them, of a humble congregation of dissenters who had fled from the very districts of their native land in which foreign heretics were tolerated, to escape the tyrannical surveillance of the Church, and who had found a refuge for a time in the great university town of Leyden. They came now to America because they did not wish their children to become Dutch or lose altogether their Eng-

lish speech and customs, and because they could look
to have an even more untrammelled freedom upon the
fruitful coasts of the New World than in the ancient
states of the Netherlands, into whose life they found
themselves thrust like those who must be always
aliens. They were Protestants, and had left England
because they could not brook the domination of her
Church; and yet the reason for their exile was as
much political as religious. Many men in England,
some of them high in the counsels of the Church itself, held the same doctrines that they held,—the doctrines which Calvin had made the creed and fundamental basis of belief among all Protestants of the
sterner sort,—and yet were not exiles, because they had
not broken, as these men had, with the discipline and
authority of the Church.

England's Protestantism had a color and character
of its own. Her " Reformation " had struck at the roots
of nothing except the authority of the Pope at Rome.
Her Church had always deemed itself national, had always held itself less subject than other churches to be
ruled by papal delegates, or turned this way or that by
the vicissitudes of continental politics and the policies
of the papal state. She had broken with Rome at last,
when the Reformation came, not because she was deeply stirred in thought and conscience by the doubts and
the principles of belief which Luther had put afloat to
the upsetting of Europe, so much as because her King,
the wilful Henry, was vexed by the restraints put upon
his marriages and divorces by the papal authority, and
therefore chose to lead her still further along upon the
road of independence to which her position and her
pride inclined her, in religion no less than in politics.

HOUSE IN PLYMOUTH, ENGLAND, WHERE THE MAYFLOWER PILGRIMS
WERE ENTERTAINED

When the change had been made, stupendous as it
looked amid the ruin of the monastic houses which
the King had promptly despoiled, Englishmen found
themselves very little more at liberty than before to choose
forms of worship or of church government for themselves.
The Church had become more than ever a part of the
state. The King was its head and master, instead of
the Pope. He did not insist very much upon matters
of doctrine, being himself in no case to set an example
in that kind; but he did insist upon the authority of the
Church in matters of government,—upon uniformity in
worship and in discipline; because the discipline of the
Church was now the discipline of the state, and part of
his own sovereignty. He deemed schism a form of disloyalty, though opinion, if it kept within discreet bounds,
he would not too curiously look into. It was an easy

enough rule. Things might have gone very quietly and with a normal growth and liberalization, had not Mary, a fanatical Catholic, become Queen, and tried forthwith to force every one in the kingdom back into the Church of Rome; had not Elizabeth, in her turn, proved so absolute a martinet in every matter of obedience to the crown,—in matters which affected the Church no less than in matters which affected only her crown and government. Mary drove those who resisted her to the stake, or out of the kingdom. Elizabeth looked shrewdly into every movement that threatened the uniformity of worship, as changes of opinion inevitably did, and saw to it that all men were turned to adopt her preference.

Most persons quietly submitted. Even men of strong convictions deemed it better to remain within the Church and purify its beliefs and practices without schism or revolution than to fling out of it, breaking both its unity and the peace of the country. Such men even drew together as a distinct party of "Puritans,"—men who wished the Church to be pure and to hold the essential doctrines of the great reformers who had given life and substance to protestantism, but who did not mean to lead it faster than it could go in the new ways, or to separate themselves from it and set up a Church and worship of their own, even though it were the excellent forms and beliefs of the church of Geneva. Others, however, were of a more exacting conscience, a more imperious and separate way of belief. It meant a great deal to them to have come into direct contact with the Word of God, to have thought upon its living sentences with the free, unbidden, individual right of interpretation of which great Luther had set the example. It

JOHN WINTHROP

was King Henry himself who had authorized the publication of the Bible in English, and who had commanded that it be made accessible everywhere in the churches; and when once they had thought upon it for themselves and had found their thought, sober and chastened as it was, running in unsanctioned channels, some men preferred their own consciences and their own views of the truth to obedience, and refused to conform. They followed the example of the Dutch, now to be found almost everywhere among them, and set up independent con-

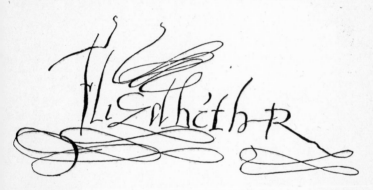

gregations,—became "Separatists," secretly and in defiance of the crown.

Elizabeth, bent upon being sovereign in all things, had grown harsher and harsher towards those who would not submit to authority in matters of belief and worship. Law upon law had been passed to prevent Englishmen from organizing any worship of their own which the bishops did not sanction; and whatever was law Elizabeth saw to it should be executed. And then, when Elizabeth was gone, James of Scotland came to the throne and completed the discomfiture and despair of those who had clung to the Church through all that had gone before, in the hope of better times and more liberal ways of government. He had seemed a veritable Presbyterian so long as he was King of Scotland; but when he became King of England also he turned out

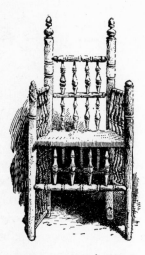

to be of another opinion. "A Scottish presbytery," he exclaimed, "agreeth as well with a monarchy as God with the devil." He was head of the Church, he declared, not only because Henry had cast loose from Rome, but also because it was of divine ordinance and appointment that he should be. The bishops of the Church were his agents. "No bishop, no King," he said; and men found that they must obey the King in matters of religion as never before.

ELDER BREWSTER'S CHAIR

It was in the disheartening days of this new tyranny that the little company of "Separatists" fled from England into Holland who were afterwards to seek new shelter within Cape Cod in America. They had waited only until there should be peace between the Netherlands and Spain; and the truce had come at last in 1609 which gave them their freedom to go, following after scores of their countrymen who had gone before them. They had formed their separate association for worship in England three years before, in defiance of the law, meeting quietly in the old manor house at Scrooby, a little hamlet just within the borders of Nottinghamshire, on the great north road from London to Edinburgh. They were humble folk, for the most part, of no social consequence, with only two or three scholars among them,—William Brewster, their elder, and John Robinson, their "teacher," and one or two others bred at Cambridge, men of strong convictions and an exalted sense of independence and duty, who had been driven from the Church for nonconformity. But, humble though they were, 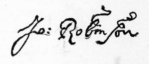 they could not keep their ways of worship hid from prying eyes. The law was rigorously enforced against them, and they soon found that they could have no peace in England.

They fled first to Amsterdam, but after about a year removed to Leyden (1609). There they made comfortable enough homes for themselves, by dint of careful thrift and hard labor. Their new neighbors liked them and helped them, because they found them capable, honest, and diligent. But it was not like being in England, after all. They felt themselves exiles all the while. Mr. Robinson, with his learning and his sweet eloquence, made friends and found congenial tasks at the university, where his gifts were recognized and honored; and Mr. Brewster established himself as a teacher, "instructing students at the university, Danes and Germans, in the English language," and even set up a printing-press, where books forbidden as heretical in England could be printed. Scholars were by breeding men of the world, and could adopt the manners and enjoy the companionships of a new country with a certain zest and relish. Mr. Brewster had known these strange places before. Close upon five-and-twenty years before, when the great war and tragic grapple with Spain was at its heat, he had come into the Netherlands with William Davison, the hard-headed Scottish Puritan whom Elizabeth was pleased to employ as her ambassador in that quarter. He counted statesmen and travellers and men about the sovereign's person among his friends, and could be well enough at ease wherever duty or employment led him. But the majority of the little band were humble folk and found their lot hard. Even a bare living was difficult to eke out in a strange country, whose manners were as unfamiliar to them as its

A PILGRIM BABY'S CRADLE

language. They saw their children growing up, too, as the years went by, in a way that threatened to make them as Dutch as their neighbors, and forfeit their nationality altogether; and that was deeply distasteful to them. When the truce approached its end, therefore, and war was again at hand, a final argument of discouragement was added, and they determined to try their fortunes in the New World, where Virginia had now become fairly established and seemed secure of its future.

They sent agents to London to speak with the managers of the Virginia Company, and obtain leave to settle within their grant. Mr. Brewster could go to Sir Edwin Sandys as to a man who knew him and would befriend him willingly. He had lived at Scrooby manor house as agent of Sir Samuel Sandys, Sir Edwin's brother, and Sir Edwin knew his integrity and was of too liberal a temper to distrust him for his independency in matters of belief and worship. The exiles could count upon favor in that quarter, now that a statesman ruled in the counsels of the great company. They did not wish to go to Jamestown or to lose in any way their separate organization as a congregation by being merged with plantations already made; and for a little, while their negotiations with the Virginia Company dragged slowly, because Sir Edwin Sandys and its other leaders were of necessity called off to other things, they thought of entering into some arrangement with the Dutch West India Company to secure a separate allotment of land near the Great North River of New Netherland. But that plan fell through, and some of them at last set forth with a charter from the Virginia Company,—a charter conceived in the liberal spirit of the men who had sent Sir George Yeardley out to give Virginia a representative assembly and the full privileges of Englishmen.

By it their leaders were authorized to associate with themselves "the gravest and discreetest" of their companions and to make for themselves such "orders, ordinances, and constitutions for the better ordering and directing of their business and servants" as they should deem best, provided only that they should ordain nothing contrary to the laws of England. They were to be from the first their own masters in making a way to succeed. Not all could go. There was not money, there were not ships enough. Sir Edwin Sandys, with his generous public spirit in such matters, loaned them three hundred pounds without interest; but they had no resources of their own, and the rest of the money they needed they were obliged to borrow from unwilling merchants who exacted the utmost usury, and made many delays about letting them have the little they consented to lend. It was the month of September, 1620, before those who could go, a hundred and two in all, got fairly upon their way, in a single small vessel, the *Mayflower*. Mr. Brewster went with them, as their leader, but Mr. Robinson stayed behind; for the greater number remained, to await a later opportunity, and wished to keep their pastor with them.

Stress of weather kept the little *Mayflower* nine weeks on the Atlantic; and when at last, in the bleak days of late November, they sighted land, it turned out to be Cape Cod, and not the Virginia coast at all. The master of the ship had let his reckonings go wrong, was many leagues north of the land-fall he had been instructed to make, by the Bay of Delaware, and found himself, as he closed with the coast he had blindly come upon, involved in shoals from which he did not very well know how safely to extricate himself. The Virginia Company had been divided into two bodies, as Mr. Brewster's people knew very well, and the gentlemen in London from whom they had got their charter had no rights over this northern coast. It belonged now to the separate "Plymouth" branch of the company. The immigrants had half a mind to make for Hudson's River, after all. But the season was late and stormy, and the captain surly and unwilling, and they determined to land where they were and make the best of what they had hit upon. They took care first, however, to have some sort of government made ready for the landing. Their charter from the Virginia Company being no longer serviceable, and a few even of their little group of settlers being

NEW ENGLISH CANAAN

OR

NEW CANAAN

Containing an Abstract of New England,

Composed in three Bookes.

The first Booke setting forth the originall of the Natives, the Manners and Customes, together with their tractable Nature and Love towards the English.

The second Booke setting forth the naturall Indowments of the Country, and what staple Commodities it yealdeth.

The third Booke setting forth, what people are planted there, their prosperity, what remarkable accidents have happened since the first planting of it, together with their Tenents and practise of their Church.

Written by Thomas Morton of Cliffords Inne gent, *upon ten yeares knowledge and experiment of the Country.*

Printed at AMSTERDAM,
By JACOB FREDERICK STAM.
In the Yeare 1 6 3 7.

TITLE-PAGE OF MORTON'S "NEW ENGLISH CANAAN"

persons taken aboard in England who were not of their congregation,—and not certain, therefore, to submit without compulsion to be governed by their authority and discipline,—they judged it best to draw up an agree-

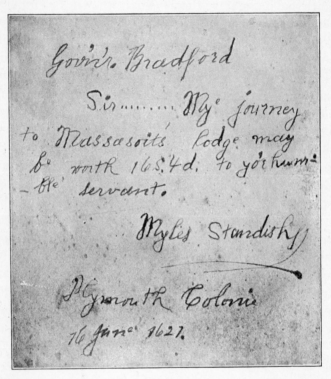

FACSIMILE OF A LETTER FROM MYLES STANDISH TO GOVERNOR BRADFORD

ment before going ashore, by which all should bind themselves to accept the authority of their leaders, until, at any rate, they should obtain a grant of lands and of power from the Plymouth Company, upon whose coasts they were thus unexpectedly to be set down. That done, they were ready to make their landing, and see what sort of a home the new coast would afford them.

The shores of the sea within Cape Cod by no means showed the soft summer aspect which Captain John Smith had found upon them in 1614, when he had cruised along these coasts. They had reminded him then of green Devonshire and the soft slopes of England. But now they were bleak and frosted and desolate. The pilgrims were not men to lose heart, however, and their leaders were of such quality as to relish difficulty and find a zest in daring. Besides Mr. Carver, who had been their agent in obtaining the Virginia charter, which they could not use, and whom they had chosen to be their governor, first under their Virginian grant and now again under the voluntary compact signed there in the ship's cabin, Captain Myles Standish was of their company, whose people had served England ever since Agincourt, and before, who had himself fought, for the love of it, against the Spaniard in the Low Countries, and who, when the fighting was over, had happened upon their little congregation at Leyden, and had chosen to cross with them to America because he liked both them and the enterprise. There was Edward Winslow, also, a young gentleman of Worcestershire, who had in like manner chanced to come upon them in his travels and had of like preference cast in his lot with them; and William Bradford, of their own humble sort, who had gone with them into Holland when but a lad of twenty, had made himself a bit of a scholar while he plied his trade as a silk-weaver, and was now, at thirty, counted already a tried man of counsel and of action.

Several weeks elapsed before a suitable place was found for landing and erecting shelter; and even then it was only "the best they could find,"—the quiet harbor, within a little bay, upon which Captain Smith had written "Plymouth" on the map he had sketched as

EDWARD WINSLOW

he passed that way, putting into bays and examining harbors with businesslike curiosity, six years before. January had come, and the first rigors of winter, before they got to work to put up shelter. Happily, the winter

A
RELATION OR

Iournall of the beginning and proceedings
of the Englifh Plantation fetled at *Plimoth* in NEW
ENGLAND, by certaine Englifh Aduenturers both
Merchants and others.

With their difficult paffage, their fafe ariuall, their
ioyfull building of, and comfortable planting them-
felues in the now well defended Towne
of NEW PLIMOTH.

AS ALSO A RELATION OF FOVRE

feuerall difcoueries fince made by fome of the
fame Englifh Planters there refident.

I. In a iourney to PVCKANOKICK *the habitation of the Indians greateft King* Maffafoyt : *as alfo their meffage, the anfwer and entertainment
they had of him.*

II. *In a voyage made by ten of them to the Kingdome of* Nawfet, *to feeke
a boy that had loft himfelfe in the woods : with fuch accidents as befell them
in that voyage.*

III. *In their iourney to the Kingdome of* Namafchet, *in defence of their
greateft King* Maffafoyt, *againft the* Narrohiggonfets, *and to reuenge the
fuppofed death of their Interpreter* Tifquantum.

IIII. *Their voyage to the* Maffachufets, *and their entertainment there.*

With an anfwer to all fuch obiections as are any way made
againft the lawfulneffe of Englifh plantations
in thofe parts.

LONDON,
Printed for *John Bellamie*, and are to be fold at his fhop at the two
Greyhounds in Cornhill neere the Royall Exchange. 1622.

TITLE-PAGE OF MOURT'S "RELATION"
The earlieft publifhed book relating to Plymouth Colony

was mild, though icy cold, for all that. The strenuous work and cruel exposure of those first weeks, which wearily lengthened into months ere spring came, and the poor and insufficient food eked out from their scant supplies, brought upon them agues, fevers, scurvy, and all the other distempers that want and exposure bring, and they saw what the settlers at Jamestown had seen of the pitiless power of the wilderness. Before that dreadful season of suffering had passed full half their number were dead, Mr. Carver among the rest, and they had seen a time when there were but six or seven sound persons among them all to care for the scores who were stricken. But they were steadfast, as always. They elected Mr. Bradford governor in the stead of Mr. Carver, and went on as they could with their fight to live. They knew of no place to which to go back, and no one asked to go with the *Mayflower* when she set sail for England again in April.

They worked against tremendous odds there on that barren coast; but they wrung a living from it almost from the first, and year by year patiently learned to succeed at the hard thing they had undertaken. It was a great burden to them that they had had to borrow large sums of money from exacting London merchants to pay for the ship that was to take them out and for the stores she was to carry. They had been obliged to take the lenders into a sort of partnership, and very soon found that they were expected to return a profit almost from the outset, working for a common store as the hapless colonists of the Virginia Company had worked till sheer failure brought them a change of system. It was many a long year before they were able to buy themselves out of that quandary and begin

GOOD
NEVVES

FROM NEWENGLAND:

OR

A true Relation of things very remarkable at the Plantation of *Plimoth*
in NEVV-ENGLAND.

Shewing the wondrous providence and good-
nes of GOD, in their preservation and continuance,
*being delivered from many apparant
deaths and dangers.*

Together with a Relation of such religious and
civill Lawes and Customes, as are in practise amongst
the *Indians*, adjoyning to them at this day. As also
*what Commodities are there to be raysed for the
maintenance of that and other Plantations in the said Country.*

Written by *E. W.* who hath borne a part in the
fore-named troubles, and there liued since
their first Arrivall.

LONDON

Printed by *I. D.* for *William Bladen* and *Iohn Bellamie*, and
are to be sold at their Shops, at the *Bible* in *Pauls* Church-
yard, and at the three Golden Lyons in Corn-hill,
neere the *Royall Exchange.* 1 6 2 4.

TITLE-PAGE OF EDWARD WINSLOW'S "GOOD NEWES"

Of plimoth plantation

And first of y occasion, and Indusments ther unto, the which that y may truly unfould, y must begine at y very roote & rise of y same. The which I shall endeuor to manefest in a plaine stile; with singuler regard unto y simple trueth in all things, at least as near as my slender Judgmente can attaine the same.

1. Chapter.

It is well knowne unto y godly, and Judicious, how euer since y first breaking out of y lighte of y gospell, in our Honourable nation of England (which was y first of nations, whom y Lord adorned ther with, after y grosse darknes of popery which had couered, & ouerspred y christian world) what warrs, & oppositions euer since satan hath raised, maintained, and continued against the saincts, from time, to time, in one sorte, or other. Some times by bloody death & cruell torments, other whiles Imprisonments, banishments, & other hard usages. As being loath his kingdom should goe downe, the truth preuaile; and y Churches of God reuerte to their anciente puritie; and recouer, their primative order, libertie, & bewtie. But when he could not preuaile by these means, against the maine truethes of y gospell, but that they began to take rooting in many places; being watered with y blooud of y martires, and blesed from heauen with a gracious encrease. He then begane to take him to his anciente strategemes, used of old against the first Christians. That when by y bloody, & barbarous persecutions of y Heathen Emperours, he could not stoppe, & subuerte the course of y gospell, but that it speedily ouerspred, with a wounderfull celeritie, the then best known parts of y world. He then begane to sow errours, heresies, and wounderfull dissentions amongst y proffessours them selues (working upon their pride, & ambition, with other corrupte passions, Incidente to all mortall men; yea to y saincts them selues in some measure) By which wofull effects followed; as not only bitter contentions, & hartburnings, schismes, with other horrible confusions. But satan tooke occasion, & aduantage therby to foyst in a number of vile ceremoneys, with many unprofitable Cannons, & decrees, which haue since been as snares, to many poore, & peaceable souls. euen to this day. So as in y anciente times, the persecuti-

PAGE FROM BRADFORD'S "HISTORY OF PLIMOTH PLANTATION."
SHOWING BRADFORD'S HANDWRITING

at last a free life for themselves. Additional settlers
came out to them in small companies, season by season;
but they were not always such persons as they wished
for. They were, too many of them, young fellows of
an irresponsible and unmanageable sort, "who little
considered whither or about what they went." It was
not until a full ten years had gone by that the little
congregation were able to fulfil their long-cherished
hope and bring over from Leyden considerable numbers
of their old-time comrades in exile; and before that
time came Mr. Robinson, their beloved pastor, whom
they had most desired, was dead.

They were not a little troubled, and even endangered,
moreover, by helpless or unmanageable neighbors:
bands of Englishmen of one sort or another,—some
mere adventurers, others sober and earnest but not
fit for the grim work of making homes or winning a
livelihood in a wilderness such as that was,—who came
to attempt settlements, or trade with the Indians, on
the great Bay of Massachusetts near by. Sometimes
it was necessary in mere pity to succor these people;
sometimes it was necessary very summarily to check
them or drive them off, lest they should make irreparable
mischief with the Indians.

Despite every difficulty, nevertheless, Mr. Bradford's
indomitable colonists made their foothold secure at
Plymouth; worked themselves free from the London
partnership; found how to get good crops, and what
sorts of crops to get, out of the unwilling soil; established
fisheries upon the near-by coasts, and trading posts here
and there among the more distant Indian tribes,—one as
far away as Kennebec, in Maine. The "Council for New
England," which represented the new company estab-

lished in England to control and develop these northern coasts once included in the Virginia grants, was very glad to encourage these their unexpected colonists at Plymouth, and sent a liberal charter out to them by the very first ship that came from England after the return of the *Mayflower;* and when they were ready to ask for more privileges,—as, for example, for leave to set up a post on the Kennebec,—very promptly gave them what they asked for. By the time their old friends from Leyden came to them, in 1630, they had reason to feel secure enough in their new home, and had only their neighbors to fear,—only the past to sadden them.

It was at first only unruly or shiftless English settlers who gave them cause for uneasiness; but they had not been long at Plymouth before they were given reason to think about the Dutch also, as jealous neighbors and rivals who might cause them serious annoyance, if nothing worse. A very cordial treaty of alliance between England and Holland had been concluded when King James died, and his son, the first Charles, came to the throne, in 1625; and there was likely, for the present at least, to be peace and good will between the two peoples. But there was no telling how long it would last, and the Dutch were meanwhile growing very numerous and strong on Hudson's River. The treaty with England had, indeed, seemed to give the Dutch West India Company fresh heart for their enterprise in New Netherland. They immediately despatched thither an active man as governor, and began to erect warehouses and batteries of good stone masonry at "Fort Amsterdam" on Manhattan Island, where guns could command some portion of the great bay of the North River and the approaches to the great river itself very handily.

The scattered families at Fort Orange and on the South River, at Fort Nassau, were brought together for greater strength and security at Fort Amsterdam, and there were presently close upon three hundred settlers there, so busy with their labor and trading that before two years had gone by under the new governor (1628) they had sent home, in two ships alone, sixty-one thousand guilders' worth of timber from the forests, and of furs bought from the northern Indians. Mr. Bradford and his people at Plymouth set up a trading post some twenty miles to the southward on Buzzards Bay, but it turned out that the Dutch could beat them there; for it was chiefly on Long Island, which the Dutch controlled, that the *wampum* was to be obtained which the Indians accepted as money, and the Plymouth traders were at a serious disadvantage without it. They were cut off from the lucrative fur trade of the North River, and were every way pushed very hard by the shrewd Dutch traders.

The governors of the rival colonies exchanged very courteous letters, and the secretary of New Netherland was sent on a visit of ceremony and good will to Plymouth; but even in this friendly correspondence there were prophetic hints of something less gentle and peaceable. Bradford called Governor Minuit's attention to the fact that the Dutch were settled within the limits of grants made by the English crown to the Virginia Company, and that their right to be there might some day be called in question; and Minuit replied, very spiritedly, "As the English claim authority under the King of England, so we derive ours from the States of Holland,

and will defend it." No doubt, too, the secretary of the Dutch colony was sent upon his visit of courtesy as much to see how the English fared and report upon the strength of the Plymouth settlement as to carry messages of good feeling. It is from him that we learn what the pilgrim colony looked like in that early day, when it was but seven years old (1627): how a broad street, it might be eight hundred feet long, ran up the hill straight from the landing place in the harbor, and was crossed midway by another street, with four cannon in the open place at the crossing, and the governor's house close by upon the upper corner; how the houses, all of good hewn plank, stood in their little gardens ranged at intervals along the streets, and stockaded against attack; and how, crowning the hill, there stood a square building, large and very stoutly made, on whose top, as on a platform, there were six cannon placed, to command from their elevation the country round about and the harbor below, and within which was their place of meeting and of worship. They went always to church in military array, he said, their captain commanding, and laid their arms down close beside them while they worshipped and heard the sermon. They remembered their sojourn in Holland with much gratitude, and accorded the Dutch secretary a hearty welcome. But it was likely that New Amsterdam and New Plymouth would be keen rivals, nevertheless, and no love lost between them in the long run.

Authorities on the history of New Netherland and New York in the seventeenth century. The first volume of John Romeyn Brodhead's *History of the State of New York* gives the history of the Dutch period in a narrative of unusual dignity, lucidity, and fulness. The second volume brings the narrative down to 1691. Edward B. O'Callaghan's *History of New Netherland*, in two volumes, is a careful and detailed narrative of the Dutch period only. Mr. John Fiske, in his *Dutch and Quaker Colonies*, sketches the whole length of New Netherland and New York history in his well-known broad and lucid way, with a wealth of incidental illustrative detail. William Smith's *History of the Late Province of New York from its Discovery to 1762* is contained in the *Collections* of the New York Historical Society. Bancroft and Hildreth both sketch the history of New York in tolerably full outline in their general histories of the country.

The *sources* of New Netherland and New York history are to be found chiefly in E. B. O'Callaghan's *Laws and Ordinances of New Netherland, 1638-1674*, and in the same author's *Documentary History of the State of New York*; in the fifteen volumes of E. B. O'Callaghan's and Berthold Fernow's *Documents Relative to the Colonial History of the State of New York*; in the *Memoirs* of the Long Island Historical Society; in the *Publications* of the Hakluyt Society; in Sainsbury's *Calendar of* [English] *State Papers, Colonial V.*; in Stedman and Hutchinson's *Library of American Literature*; in the *Appendix* to Read's *Henry Hudson*; and in the *Records of New Netherland from 1653 to 1674*, edited by Berthold Fernow.

Authorities on the history of New Plymouth in the seventeenth century. John Gorham Palfrey's *History of New England* (1492-1774) and *Compendious History of New England* (1497-1765), the former in five and the latter in four volumes, are the standard general histories of the group of colonies of which Plymouth was the first. Mr. J. A. Doyle, in the second volume of his *English Colonies in America*, gives an excellent account of the Plymouth colony in the modern critical method. Mr. John Fiske sketches its history in his *Beginnings of New England*. Bancroft and Hildreth set it forth at some length in their histories. Mr. F. B. Dexter gives a brief critical sketch of it in the third volume of Winsor's *Narrative and Critical History of America*.

The *original sources* of the narrative are to be found, for the most part, in William Bradford's *History of the Plymouth Plantation*, always admirable for its accuracy and good temper, which brings the account down at first hand to 1647; in the *Plymouth Colony Records*; in the *Collections* of the Massachusetts Historical Society; in Alexander Young's *Chronicles of the Pilgrim Fathers* and *Chronicles of Massachusetts*; and in Stedman and Hutchinson's *Library of American Literature*.

For accounts of the general Puritan movement in England of which the Plymouth emigration formed a part, see the references following Section III. of this chapter.

III. The Massachusetts Company

THE business of both Church and State had altered very ominously in England during the eventful years which brought James's reign to a close and gave Englishmen their first taste of Charles's quality. The air had filled with signs of revolution; and it was one of the most serious of these that the Puritans, who had once been merely champions of pure doctrine and a simplified worship within the Church, had now become a political party, and were trying to put a curb upon the King in every matter. At first they had thought that they might reform the Church, which they loyally loved, by the slow and peaceable ways of precept and example,—by preaching the new doctrines of Calvin, and by systematically simplifying the worship in their churches until they should have got the forms and notions of Rome out of them altogether. Elizabeth taught them that that was impossible while she was queen. Her harsh measures hardened their temper, and made them a distinct and active party: first for concert within the Church; now at last for concert also in matters of state, because the times had changed.

James had come to the throne and grievously disappointed them; and Charles, after him, had turned out to be not even a serious opponent of Rome itself. In 1618, while James was yet king, the terrible Thirty Years' War had come, that mighty struggle between the Prot-

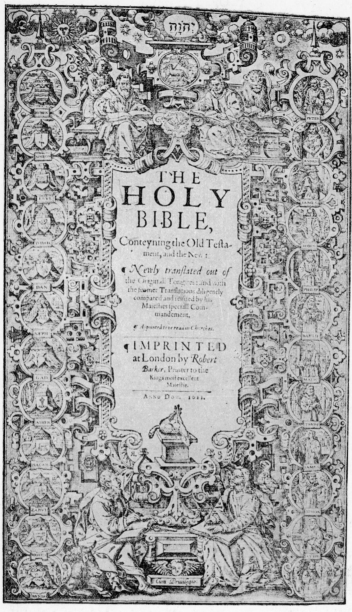

THE
HOLY
BIBLE,

Conteyning the Old Testament, and the New:

Newly translated out of the Originall Tongues: and with the former Translations diligently compared and reuised by his Maiesties speciall Commandement,

Appointed to be read in Churches.

IMPRINTED at London by Robert Barker, Printer to the Kings most excellent Maiestie.

ANNO DOM. 1611.

Cum Priuilegio.

TITLE-PAGE OF FIRST EDITION OF KING JAMES'S BIBLE

estant and the Roman Catholic states of the Continent, which threatened to tear away the very foundations of liberty and of national life, should the papacy prevail; and yet Charles had married a Roman Catholic princess, and showed himself as ready to make bargains with Roman Catholic as alliances with Protestant princes. Moreover, he was as indifferent to the political rights of his subjects as he was to their Protestant opinions. When his Parliament, disapproving his policy, refused to vote him money, he levied taxes without their consent, and seemed determined to break as he pleased every understanding of the constitution. The salvation of the Church and the salvation of the liberties of England he made to seem one and the same thing: for he would respect neither law nor opinion. And so the chief Puritan gentlemen of the kingdom became politicians, and filled the House of Commons with men of their way of thinking, grimly determined to make a single piece of work of the purification of the Church and the maintenance of liberty. Charles found no way to be rid of their protests except to do without a Parliament altogether; and to that at last he made up his mind. He dismissed the Parliament of 1629, resolved to have done with Parliaments. For eleven years he kept his resolve. No Parliament was summoned; money was raised without warrant of law; and the government was conducted entirely as he willed.

It was in that way he brought a great revolution on and lost his head, for he was dealing with men who could not safely be defied. But for the moment he seemed master. The first shock of such events was enough to dismay men who were lovers of law and of right, who had intended no revolution, who had meant to fight tyranny only by legal process and in behalf of privileges acknowledged time out of mind. Even stout-

John Calvin JOHN CALVIN

hearted men lost hope for a little, and thought their cause undone in that dark year 1629, when they saw their leaders in the King's prisons, and the King masterful and hot against all who dared so much as protest. And so a new exodus began, not to Holland this time, but direct to America,—an exodus not of separatists, of whom the law had already made outlaws, but of those sober Puritans who had remained in the Church, and had been its hope of reform.

A company had been formed among them for the purpose of attempting a settlement in America even before the end of all Puritan hopes had seemed to come. Lands had been purchased from the Council for New England in March, 1628, and a party of settlers had been sent out that very summer under John Endecott, a blunt, passionate, wilful man, hard to deal with, but more efficient than any other the company could find, and more likely to succeed. He chose Salem, not far within the northern cape of the great Bay of Massachusetts, as his place of settlement; and when a large body of new settlers were sent out to him the next summer he and his people were ready for them, with houses built and crops ripening. That same year, 1629, the company in England obtained a charter from the crown, and assumed a new importance and authority as "The Governor and Company of Massachusetts Bay in New England."

There could have been no better time to get recruits for a Puritan colony,—not mechanics merely, and such humble folk, or men out of employment, but people of substance also, who would give themselves and their fortunes to the enterprise, in the hope that they might at any rate find freedom of conscience, and establish a free state in America. Most of those who entered the company meant also to become its colonists. The company itself, therefore, was transferred over sea, its governor and council themselves taking ship to the colony they were to govern. There was not to be a

"Governor and Company of Massachusetts Bay" set up in London to rule and dispose of a distant colony, as the Virginia Company had ruled Virginia. It was

JOHN ENDECOTT

to have its seat where it had its possessions. It kept still a group of its incorporators in London, organized for the management of its financial interests; and the law officers of the crown no doubt for a time deemed these the council of the company itself. But they learned presently that they were not. The real rulers of the new colony had no mind to conduct their business in London in open courts under the eye of the King and draw all the talk of the town upon them, as the Virginia Company had done, to its undoing. There was nothing in their charter which prescribed where the councils of the company should meet. They made bold, therefore, to take their charter and all the business done under it with them to America. More than seventeen ships and a thousand colonists got away from the western and southern seaports,—Bristol, Plymouth, Weymouth, Southampton,—in the spring and summer of 1630, Mr. John Winthrop, a man of gentle breeding, of education, of private means, and of the high principles of the best Puritan tradition, a man trained to the law, and, what was much better, schooled in a firm but moderate temper, sweet yet commanding, going out as governor to supersede Endecott. Thomas Dudley went as his deputy, a man cast in another mould, and of another type, a doughty Puritan soldier who had served under Henry of Navarre; an uncompromising partisan, more man-at-arms than statesman.

Want and disease had done their accustomed work among Endecott's people before the new governor and company reached the Bay. Mr. Higginson, who had written them from Salem scarcely a year ago that "a sup of New England's air was better than a whole draught of old England's ale," was hardly able to stand to preach to them when they landed, a fatal fever having taken hold upon him. It was necessary to separate at once and begin other settlements where Mr. Winthrop's

NEW-ENGLANDS
PLANTATION.

OR,
A SHORT AND TRVE
DESCRIPTION OF THE
COMMODITIES AND
DISCOMMODITIES
of that Countrey.

Written by a reuerend Diuine now
there resident.

Higgeson.

LONDON,
Printed by *T.C.* and *R.C.* for *Michael Sparke,*
dwelling at the Signe of the *Blew Bible* in
Greene Arbor in the little *Old Bailey.*
1630.

TITLE-PAGE OF FRANCIS HIGGINSON'S BOOK

people might prepare shelter for the winter. As soon as possible, therefore, places were chosen. Watertown, Roxbury, Boston, Dorchester were begun, and the preparation of Charlestown, already begun before their coming, was pushed forward, — all places far within the Bay, where groups of sheltering islands shouldered out the heavier seas, and harbors were quiet. But the work was sadly belated. Autumn had come and was gone before much could be accomplished. A full hundred of the immigrants lost heart and went back with the ships to England. Winter found those who remained short of food and still without sufficient shelter, and want and disease claimed two hundred victims among them. Even the ships they despatched hastily to England for corn brought very little when they came again, for grain was scarce and dear at home also.

With the spring came health and hope again, as always; but bad news, too. Those who had returned home disheartened had spread damaging reports about the colony, not only telling of the sore straits it was in to live, but also declaring that Mr. Winthrop and his people had openly repudiated the Church of England and turned separatists, like the people at Plymouth. It was difficult to quiet these reports, because they were practically true. It was not easy to explain away what had undoubtedly been done. Both the immigrants with Mr. Endecott at Salem and those who had come with Mr. Winthrop had left home members of the Church of England: Puritans and reformers, indeed, but still not separatists, and publicly professing a warm loyalty for the mother Church. "We esteem it an honor," they had said, as they uttered their final partings at Yarmouth, "to call the Church of England, from whence we rise, our dear mother." "We shall always rejoice in her good, . . . and while we have breath sincerely desire and endeavor the continuance and abundance of

MYLES STANDISH

her welfare, with the enlargement of her bounds." And yet Endecott had hardly begun his settlement at Salem before he took counsel with Mr. Brewster and other leaders at Plymouth, and rearranged both the worship and the government of his church after their model. Mr. Winthrop's people had done the same. Those who protested and showed themselves unwilling to accept the new ways of church government were compelled either to conform or return home to England. The whole thing looked like the carrying out of a deliberate plan made beforehand to get rid of the Church as well as of the government of England: to set up a separate church along with a separate commonwealth.

They could hardly say that it was the necessary result of their removal to a distant continent; for the numerous body of Englishmen long ago settled in Virginia had done nothing of the sort, though they maintained their own churches. The Virginians had remained staunch supporters of the Church as it was at home. Their own assembly had passed strict laws to enforce the accustomed discipline of the English Church and to protect its forms of worship. It could not be said that they did not love their freedom as much as the settlers at Plymouth and the Bay loved theirs. They were glad enough to have an ocean between them and the bishops, did not hesitate to discard the surplice, simplified their worship as they pleased, and took leave to make very free use of the opportunity to rule their own affairs. But they loved none the less the ancient Church in which they had been bred, and they meant to maintain it.

Virginia had been planted before the full warmth of the Puritan temper had made itself felt in England, when it was esteemed a reproach to be called a separatist, and a proud duty which went along with a man's allegiance to hold fast to the standards of the nation's

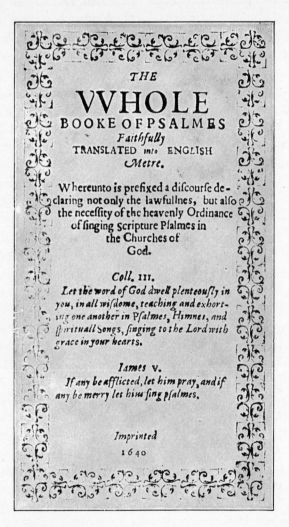

THE

VVHOLE

BOOKE OF PSALMES

Faithfully

TRANSLATED *into* ENGLISH

Metre.

Whereunto is prefixed a difcourfe declaring not only the lawfullnes, but alfo
the neceffity of the heavenly Ordinance
of finging Scripture Pfalmes in
the Churches of
God.

Coll. III.

*Let the word of God dwell plenteoufly in
you, in all wifdome, teaching and exhort-
ing one another in Pfalmes, Himnes, and
fpirituall Songs, finging to the Lord with
grace in your hearts.*

Iames V.

*If any be afflicted, let him pray, and if
any be merry let him fing pfalmes.*

Imprinted

1640

TITLE-PAGE OF THE "BAY PSALM BOOK"

Church. Virginia had been recruited, too, as she grew, not out of a special class like the Puritans, with a cause at their hearts, but out of the general body of the English people, in whose lives and thoughts the disputes which grew so keen from year to year within the Church played very little part. They had brought their religious beliefs and their forms of worship with them to Virginia as habits in their blood, unseparated and undistinguished from their English citizenship. The new settlers on Massachusetts Bay, on the contrary, had been selected out of a special class. They were men bent for conscience' sake upon setting up a particular standard of their own both in church and in state. They had a deliberate plan from the first to withdraw themselves from the general body of Englishmen and establish in America what should seem to them "a due form of government, both civil and ecclesiastical." "God sifted a whole nation that He might send choice grain out into this wilderness," one of their own preachers said. They tried to explain away their novel proceedings when they wrote to persons of influence at home; they tried to persuade even themselves that they were not separatists, but only a distant and necessarily distinct fragment of the Church of England, of the form which they hoped and expected to see that great Church some day assume; but they were, in fact, founding a separate establishment which denied the authority of the mother Church altogether.

Virginia had slowly grown to a population of five thousand while the Puritans organized their company and transported it to America. Virginians bore themselves very much as Englishmen did everywhere. There

A VIRGINIA PLANTER WITH HIS ATTENDANTS IN HIS BOAT ON THE
JAMES RIVER

—8

was nothing peculiar about them except their hardihood, as of frontiersmen, and their knowledge of how life was to be managed and set forward in a wilderness. It had not made much difference among them that the Virginia Company was dissolved and the colony put into the hands of the King. For the first four years that followed the change no assemblies were summoned, it is true, and they were ruled by the governors and the governors' councils whom the King appointed. But the governors chosen by the King during those years were men of their own number, their trusted friends, already experienced in their affairs, men whom the company also had employed. Leading men of the colony were appointed to the council also. The general interest was consulted, though there were no elections. Before a governor not to the people's taste was put over them the old practice of calling assemblies had been resumed. Virginians wished their individual rights to be left untouched, and watched their government narrowly to see that it did not impose upon them; but their life went well enough, and they were not disposed to seek radical changes either in church or state.

They were not settled in close groups, and were not always discussing their common affairs, as men do who live together in towns or organize themselves in compact neighborhoods for business. There was no real town in the colony, except Jamestown. The homes of the colony were scattered through wide neighborhoods along the margins of the rivers, which flowed broad and deep and from every quarter, the natural highways of the place. Each planter farmed as much of the fertile land as he could; but he planted little for sale

DUTCH WEST INDIA COMPANY'S HOUSE, HAARLEM STREET,
AMSTERDAM

except tobacco. His tobacco he shipped away in vessels
which came to his own wharf and the wharves of his
neighbors to be laden. It was not hard to live in that
genial climate. Great clearings had at last been made;

the sun had been let wholesomely in to take the fever-
ish vapors of the forest off, and the land had begun to
yield health as well as abundance.   Secluded country
churches were the neighborhood gathering places of the
colony, for talk as well as for worship.   Planters made
their way to Jamestown down the rivers in their own
boats, or through the quiet paths of the forest on horse-
back, to be present at the gathering of the assembly,
or to attend the quarterly meetings of the governor's
council, at which lawsuits were heard and determined.
It was all a leisurely way of life, and was not apt to
bring changes rapidly about so long as the King suffered
them to enjoy their reasonable liberty as Englishmen
and did not put men who wished to rule overmuch into
their governor's chair.

New Netherland grew also, in a way which might
have looked to a chance visitor very like the growth of
Virginia.   The Dutch West India Company had found
that if they kept to the plan with which they had begun,
they could not hope to make anything more than a mere
trading station out of their slow-growing settlement at
Fort Amsterdam.   The council of the company, accordingly, determined to offer large tracts of land to
any one who would send over at his own cost fifty
adult settlers, with stores and equipment,—and with
the land extraordinary powers of independent control,
which should constitute the owner a sort of feudal prince,
as "patroon" and lord of his estate.   The offer had in it
the enticing prospect of dignity and power and safe
wealth, such as the landed gentry of Holland had time
out of mind enjoyed and the merchants of the towns had
envied them as long, and some were tempted, as the

company had hoped. Some rich men did bestir themselves to send settlers over, and great stretches of the best land on both the North and the South rivers of New Netherland were presently made over to private owners. It was no easier, however, for private individuals than it had been for the company to bring the land success-

ENGLISH GENTLEMAN,
1633

ENGLISH GENTLEWOMAN,
1631

fully under cultivation, or to establish settlements which would thrive and endure; and the new way of building up the colony went as slowly as the old. Many of the new proprietors failed; only a few succeeded. The most notable of the estates which were actually peopled and established was that of Kilian van Rensselaer, the wealthy jeweller of Amsterdam, which stretched for miles upon either bank of the North River in the fertile region far up the stream where the company's Fort Orange stood, and where the heart of the fur trade with the Indians was.

Even where this new way of growth succeeded, however, it was in fact very different from the slow and natural spread of broad plantations in Virginia, where no man was by law more privileged than another. The Dutch farmers and peasants who slowly filled the estates of the patroons with tenants were not like the free

SIGNATURE OF KILIAN VAN RENSSELAER, PATROON

yeomen of the southern colony of the English. They were just as little like the New England colonists to the northward. Among these settlement had still another way of growth. They did not develop by the slow spreading of private estates along the river valleys. The New England valleys were not fertile; the rivers were not deep or broad enough to be the highways of the colony. The sort of government the Puritan settlers wished to maintain, moreover, would have been almost impossible had the people not kept together in close groups for common action and worship. The governor and company who ruled Massachusetts Bay governed there very watchfully in the midst of the settlements, and took care to know the men to whom they made grants of land. Sometimes they made grants to individuals for special services or liberal contributions to the company's funds; but usually they gave land only to bands of settlers who meant to form communities, and who were under the leadership of persons whom the governor and his associates trusted. The new settlers of each locality owned their lands jointly, as if they were a corporation. Their "town meeting" determined what portion each individual among them was to have for his own use. No other settlers could join them unless admitted by their town meeting to the partnership. All local affairs were managed by officers whom the town meeting elected. Each town, the newest no less than Salem or Charlestown or Roxbury or Boston, was its own mistress, except when matters which the company determined in the common interest were to be acted on.

In each town there were "selectmen" chosen to administer the general business of the town; constables to keep order; cowherds to take the cattle to the common pasture, keep them there while their owners did their tasks through the day, and bring them back at sunset; swineherds to drive the swine to their feeding and return them safe in the evening; a hayward to catch stray beasts and keep them fast till they were claimed: a man for each simple duty. The swineherd made his way along the village streets early in the morning, sounding his horn, and every man who had swine brought them out to him at the summons to join his noisy procession, going forth to the woods for their feeding for the day. The cowherd took all his lowing charges to pasture from a common pen, to which their owners brought them in the grey of the dawn, and was charged

FACSIMILE OF ORDER CREATING BOARD OF SELECTMEN,
CHARLESTOWN, 1634

to be back with them ere the sun should set. The town meeting decided all things, small and great. It did not hesitate to order in what way the houses should be set and roofed and distributed along the street, and their gardens disposed about them. In Newtown the free-men ordered by vote that all houses within the village "be covered with slate or board, and not with thatch," and that they be built so that they should "range even" and stand just six feet from the street. Every freeman and proprietor of the village had his vote in the meet-ing, and deemed himself self - governed when it gov-erned him.

The government of the colony as a whole was by no means so democratic. The "company" governed; and the company consisted only of those who were admitted as "freemen" by its own vote. At first there were only twenty such among all the thousand settlers at the Bay, and twelve of these twenty were the officers of the com-pany. By slow degrees the number was enlarged; but the company was very reluctant and very cautious about increasing its membership. Four years went by before there were so many as three hundred and fifty "freemen," and by that time there were more than three thousand settlers. The new and very severe rule was adopted that no one should be chosen a freeman who was not a member of some one of the churches of the settlements. In England every subject was reckoned by law a member of the Church of England; but in Massa-chusetts men became members of the churches only by profession of faith and upon a searching examination in matters of doctrine and worship. Those who did not hold the strict creed of the Puritan ministers, being ex-cluded from the church, were excluded also from voting.

"The best part is always the least," was Mr. Winthrop's sententious doctrine, "and of that best part the wiser part is always the lesser."

The rule of doctrine and church authority did not stop with a restriction in the number of freemen who should vote in the company's general court. Men were fined, whipped, sentenced to have their ears cut off, or banished the colony altogether for speaking scandalously of either the church or the government. Several who had come to the Bay before the Massachusetts Company was formed were so put upon and sought out for prosecution by their new masters, the magistrates of the company, for their refusal to conform to the new practices in matters of worship, that they finally resisted to the length of bringing sentence of banishment upon themselves, or voluntarily took themselves off to escape the searching tyranny. It was a very rigorous government, under which only those could live and be at ease who professed and proved themselves Puritans; and common men suffered more than gentlemen, after the manner of the age, so that it seemed an aristocratic as well as an ecclesiastical establishment.

The King and his ministers over sea did not fail to observe how the company made its colony a stronghold for the obstructive Puritans. The temper of Charles's government grew harsher and harsher during those first years of settlement at the Bay, and became as meddlesome and tyrannical in the management of the Church as in the management of the State. In 1633 he had made Laud Archbishop of Canterbury. Now he was backing the implacable primate in a thorough-going and pitiless attempt to clear the Church of all Puritans and nonconformists. Laud was quick to see

W: Cant:

WILLIAM LAUD,
ARCHBISHOP OF CANTERBURY

what comfort the rapidly growing colony at Massachusetts Bay gave his enemies, and complained very hotly that it was filling up with persons openly hostile to the King's government. Certain persons connected with the old Council for New England, jealous of the

123

prosperous company at the Bay, with its independent royal charter, easily persuaded the all-powerful archbishop, and through him the law officers of the crown, to take steps to destroy it; and in 1635 the blow came. A judgment was obtained against the Massachusetts charter in the court of King's Bench; the government of the colony was declared transferred into the King's hands, as the government of Virginia had been, and orders were issued which authorized the despatch of a governor-general, to be accompanied, if necessary, by an armed force. Mr. Cradock, who presided over the company's financial board in London, had been summoned by the imperious primate and by my lord Privy Seal to come before them for an explanation, and bring the charter of the company with him; and had been rated very roundly as an "imposturous knave" when he declared that it had been sent over sea with the colonists. But the spiriting away of its charter had not been allowed to stay the judgment against the company.

The magistrates at the Bay, when the ugly news reached them, came to the desperate resolution to resist by force. But troubles in England saved them. Their charter was, indeed, in law annulled, but the judgment was not carried out. The King's purse was empty. His subjects were very slow about paying the illegal taxes he demanded of them. Signs of revolution were growing more and more frequent, more and more open and ominous. Charles could not afford to send an expensive expedition out to New England, and was much too anxious about things at home to think very often about the little group of troublesome settlements across the sea. Mr. Winthrop and his associates, accordingly, lived quietly on under their forfeited charter, as if nothing had happened, and admitted no one they did not like to the partnership.

An introduction to the various phases of *the Puritan movement* in England, which led to the Puritan exodus to America, may be got in G. H. Curteis's *Dissent in its Relation to the Church of England* (the Bampton lectures for 1871); in David Masson's *Life and Times of Milton* ; in D. Neal's *History of the Puritans* ; in Samuel R. Gardiner's *History of England from the Accession of James I.*, volumes I. and IV. ; in the second volume of J. R. Green's *History of the English People* ; in G. E. Ellis's *Puritan Age and Rule* ; and in the second volume of J. A. Doyle's *English Colonies in America*.

The leading *general authorities* on the history of Massachusetts in the seventeenth century are John Gorham Palfrey's *History of New England* (1492-1774) and *Compendious History of New England* (1497-1765); J. A. Doyle's second and third volumes on *The English Colonies in America* ; John Fiske's *Beginnings of New England* ; S. R. Drake's *The Making of New England* ; and Justin Winsor's *Memorial History of Boston*.

Glimpses of some of the most important special aspects of Massachusetts history are to be had in W. B. Weeden's *Economic and Social History of New England* ; Charles Francis Adams's *Three Episodes of Massachusetts History;* and Herbert B. Adams's *Germanic Origin of the New England Towns*, published in the first volume of the *Johns Hopkins University Studies in Historical and Political Science*.

Most of the important *original sources* of Massachusetts history are brought together in John Winthrop's *History of New England*, edited by J. Savage and *The Life and Letters of John Winthrop*, edited by R. C. Winthrop ; in the *Collections* and *Proceedings* of the Massachusetts Historical Society; in Alexander Young's *Chronicles of Massachusetts* ; in the *Records of the Governor and Company of the Massachusetts Bay* ; in Peter Force's *Tracts and Other Papers relating to the Colonies in North America* ; in the *Publications* of the Prince Society ; in the papers of the American Antiquarian Society ; and in the *New Hampshire Historical Collections*.

IT was a thing for statesmen to take note of, and all
to wonder at, how Englishmen of all sorts and creeds
began to think of America, and to desire homes there,
when once it had become evident that Virginia and
Plymouth and the Massachusetts settlements were
certainly permanent, and colonization no mere scheme
of the foolhardy. There were others besides the Puritans
who felt uneasy at home in England because of the
troubles in church and state and the threatening face
of affairs. For men who loved novelty and adventure,
life in the New World had always a charm which even
direst hardship could not take away; but such men
were nowhere in a majority, and it was not mere love of
adventure that made the English swarm to America.
It was the spirit of liberty and of mastery. It was the
most spirited men who were the most uneasy in those
evil days of the Stuart kings; and because they were
cramped and thwarted and humbled at home they
thought the more often and the more wistfully of the
freedom they might find in America. Virginia had
been planted and had thriven, it is true, before there
was this sting of uneasiness to drive men over sea.
She had been created because of the spirit of trade and
of conquest, the impulse of international rivalry, the
love of gain, and the capacity for independent action
which had come to Englishmen in the stirring sixteenth
century; and it was, after all, that "ancient, primitive,

and heroic work of planting the world" which was to prove the permanent motive of English success in America. But now, for the time being, there was added to

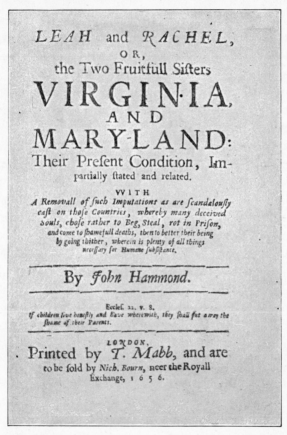

LEAH and RACHEL,
OR,
the Two Fruitfull Sisters
VIRGIN·IA,
AND
MARY·LAND:
Their Present Condition, Impartially stated and related.

WITH
A Removall of such Imputations as are scandalously cast on those Countries, whereby many deceived Souls, chose rather to Beg, Steal, rot in Prison, and come to shamefull deaths, then to better their being by going thither, wherein is plenty of all things necessary for Humane subsistance.

By John Hammond.

Ecclef. 11. v. 8.
If children live honestly and have wherewith, they shall put away the shame of their Parents.

LONDON,
Printed by T. Mabb, and are to be sold by Nich. Bourn, neer the Royall Exchange, 1 6 5 6.

TITLE-PAGE OF HAMMOND'S "LEAH AND RACHEL"

the high spirit of mastery the unquiet spirit of discontent, and America reaped a double harvest.

It happened that Roman Catholics felt almost as uneasy as Puritans. James, it was true, had proved himself no Presbyterian, after all, and Charles had put Laud at the head of the Church, as if to carry it back as far as possible towards Rome, if not all the way to Rome itself. But it needed no seer to perceive how the temper of the nation darkened at sight of these things, and no thoughtful Roman Catholic could find sound reason to hope for a long period of toleration. America would no doubt prove a freer place for Roman Catholics as well as for Puritans, and their exodus began the very year Laud became primate. It was for them that Maryland was founded by Cecilius Calvert, Lord Baltimore. It was a scheme he had inherited from his father. Sir George Calvert had been a very noticeable figure when James was king. He had stood in the Commons, alongside Wentworth, his friend, as spokesman for the King, whose intimate companion and devoted servant all knew him to be, facing Sir Edwin Sandys there, to whom the House had looked for leadership since it began to fear that James meant some deep mischief to the liberties of England. There was much to admire in his courtesy, his tact and moderation, his unobtrusive devotion to affairs. He had none of Wentworth's striking initiative and vigor, and showed a modesty, gentleness, and acquiescence in the service of the court which seemed mere weakness to those who looked on; and yet he was greatly trusted and won deep esteem. The opponents of the crown in Parliament thought him servile, and suspected him of being corrupt, like the rest of the King's agents; but those who knew him said that he acted upon conviction in making choice which side he should take, and both in public and in private bore himself like a man of honor.

GEORGE CALVERT

In the last year of the reign he had resigned his offices and withdrawn from the King's service, while still in his prime. He had become a convert to Roman Catholicism, had committed himself with the energy of real conviction to bringing about the marriage of Prince Charles to the princess of Spain, and would not draw back to please either the prince himself or great Buckingham, because he deemed both the cause of Catholicism and the plighted word of England, given in solemn treaty, involved in the project. His position at court had become untenable, and he withdrew both to save his interest and to give candid expression to his religious convictions. James had created him Baron Baltimore at parting, as a special evidence of his good will, and then Calvert had turned to devote himself to plans of colonization. He had been a large subscriber to the funds of the East India Company, had become a member of the New England Company, and had served on the commission appointed in 1624 to wind up the affairs of the great Virginia Company. As far back as 1620 he had interested himself in colonizing schemes of his own, while he was yet in the midst of affairs,—before Plymouth was founded. He had bought an extensive tract of land lying on the southern peninsula of Newfoundland; had put colonists upon it; and when he turned from holding office under the King, had himself gone to reside among his settlers.

But a single year in that rigorous climate, with its icy cold from October to May, convinced him it was no place in which to build a colony, especially with the French near at hand to be reckoned with, in addition to the weather. The French upon the near-by coasts had not forgotten how Captain Argall had put in at their struggling settlements and burned them, scarcely ten years ago, carrying off cattle and settlers alike as his prize of private war, and meant to have no English for neighbors if they could find means to drive them off. Calvert had stayed his year out at "Avalon" only because his ships were as heavily armed and better handled. The bleak land with "a sad fare of winter" upon it, which let no blade of herbage appear in the earth, nor any fish even in the sea, for close upon eight months together, seemed hardly worth fighting for.

He turned his thoughts southward, therefore, and in 1629,—the very year Parliaments ceased to sit and the Massachusetts people got their charter, — asked King Charles to grant them lands on either side the great Bay of Chesapeake, close by Virginia: from the Potomac northward and eastward, across the Bay, to the fortieth degree of north latitude and the river and bay of Delaware. All this was land granted long ago to the Virginia Company; but the Virginia Company was dead; the King had resumed his sovereign rights with the withdrawal of its charter,—cared very little whether he twice granted the same thing or not,—and was Calvert's friend, as his father had been before him. The Virginian colonists were hot against the grant, and many influential persons in England, who seemed to hope still to see the old Virginia Company revived, protested to the Privy Council against it. But though they held the matter off for a year and a half, until Calvert was dead, they did not prevent it. The charter was issued in 1632, and Cecilius Calvert, the second Lord Baltimore, carried out his father's plans in his father's spirit.

It had been evident from the first that George Calvert

had meant his colony to be, among other things, a place
of refuge, freedom, and safety for men of his own faith.
There had long been stories afloat in London how he
had carried Romish priests with him to Newfoundland,
and had celebrated mass there every Sunday. He had
named his colony there Avalon because it was at Glas-
tonbury, which men had once called Avalon, in old Somersetshire, that the Church of Rome had first set up
her altars in Britain. The colonists whom Cecilius
Calvert sent out to Maryland late in the autumn of 1633
were by no means all Romanists, but probably quite
half of them were; and Jesuit priests, who had covertly
come aboard after the ships left the Thames, went with
them to act as their spiritual leaders and preceptors in
the New World. Protestants and Catholics, however,
consorted very comfortably together on the voyage and
after the landing. It was no part of Lord Baltimore's
purpose to be a proselytizer and make converts of all
whom he sent out, and he was too cool and prudent a
man to wish to set up a colony to which none but
Roman Catholics should be admitted. He knew very
well how all England would soon be talking and protesting about such a colony as that, should he attempt
it. He meant only to make a place so free that Roman
Catholics might use full liberty of worship there no less
than Protestants, for he knew that there was as yet no
such place in America.

His colonists reached their new home in March, 1634,
and chose for their place of settlement a high bluff which
rose upon the eastern bank of a little stream which
emptied itself into the great Potomac but a little way
from the Bay. The mighty Potomac, flowing silent
between its wide banks there in the lonely wilderness,

THE SECOND LORD BALTIMORE

made a deep impression on them. "The Thames, compared with it," they said, "can scarcely be considered a rivulet. It is not rendered impure by marshes, but on each bank of solid earth rise beautiful groves of trees, not choked up with an undergrowth of brambles and bushes, but as if laid out by the hand, in a manner so open that you might easily drive a four-horse chariot in the midst of the trees." It was this broad and stately stream which was to be their boundary line, separating them from Virginia. Lord Baltimore called his province Maryland, in honor of the queen, and the first settlement there on the bluff they called St. Mary's, in honor of the Virgin.

It was a very bitter thing to the Virginians that they should be obliged thus to give up all the fair region of the upper Bay to these new-comers, whom they disliked equally as intruders and as papists; and feeling ran so high among them against Lord Baltimore's people that they deemed it an intolerable sort of treason for any man to speak so much as a kind word concerning them. They knew that they might themselves once have had all the Bay for the taking, and now the King had granted it away forever. They had, indeed, established a trading outpost on Kent's Island, which lay within reach of the spreading stream of the great Susquehanna, the noble river which brought its waters to the Bay all the long way which lay between Virginia and the forest haunts of the mighty Iroquois at the north,—the forests whence the rich furs came which all the continent coveted. Mr. Clayborne, who was of the governor's council, had interested himself to make commerce there with the natives; and Mr. Clayborne, with his good estates and high credit in Virginia, his influential commercial connections in London, his indomitable will and strong relish for action, was an ill man to oust. He insisted not only upon his own rights of property in the island, which no man of Lord

133

Baltimore's interest would have denied or interfered with, but also upon Virginia's jurisdiction over it. There could be no questioning the fact, nevertheless, that the island lay within the King's new grant; and though Mr. Clayborne begged aid of the Privy Council at home, and even put arms into the hands of his servants to keep his own by force, it was of no avail. The King's grant made Lord Baltimore master, and Mr. Clayborne had to stomach as best he could the unpalatable necessity of submitting.

Maryland's settlers had come to stay, and yearly spread and multiplied; and the Virginians in due time let their anger cool. Singular good fortune and provident good management made them secure from the first against any starving time such as there had been at Jamestown, or any bitter struggle to live and make a beginning. They had found an Indian village at St. Mary's where they landed, long established and set in the midst of open fields cultivated and ready for the plough. The Indians whose home the place had been freely sold them both its wigwams and its fallow clearings, for a few hatchets and hoes and a little cloth. Before the white men came they had resolved to quit the region, to be rid of fear of the Susquehannocks, the terrible Iroquois neighbors whose inroads made peace impossible. Here were cornfields ready for the planting, therefore, and the very first autumn of their stay in that wide wilderness the new colonists had grain enough to send a shipload to New England, to be exchanged for salt codfish. The Virginians, for all they hated them, did not refuse to sell them cattle and swine at a profit; and want was not an enemy they needed to reckon with.

Maryland turned out another Virginia in its ways

of life and government. In form, indeed, its government was very different. The King had no direct authority there. Lord Baltimore was made by his charter literally proprietor of the colony,—a sort of feudal prince, from whom, and not from the King, all titles and all authority were to be derived. He was empowered to confer rank even, and set up a kind of nobility, should he choose; and though his charter obliged him to submit such laws and regulations as he might think best to impose upon his province to the approval of the freemen of the colony, or their deputies, "called together for the framing of laws," that need have restrained him little more than the King was restrained by the Parliament at home. He could create "manors," also, with their separate courts, and proprietors as independent, almost, as the barons of old; and as the colony grew he did bestow here and there, upon a few of the richer men among his colonists, these greater gifts of privilege. The King had meant to reproduce in him the ancient powers of the stout churchmen who had kept the northern border against the Scot, and had had their separate sovereignty, as if of independent princes, for reward, making of their majestic cathedral on the high banks of Wear—

> "Half house of God,
> Half castle 'gainst the Scot."

He was to have, said his charter, "as ample rights, jurisdictions, privileges, prerogatives, royalties, liberties, immunities, and royal rights as any bishop of Durham within the bishopric or county palatine of Durham, within our kingdom of England."

But, notwithstanding his power was so great on paper,

he did not in fact use it to give the colony a character apart. Assemblies of the freemen met and made terms with the proprietor in Maryland as they had met and made terms with the company in Virginia. At first, while all the settlers were still within easy reach of St. Mary's, there were no elections. The freemen came themselves instead of choosing representatives. It was only by slow degrees that a system of elections was established. But in the end things were arranged there very much as they were arranged in Virginia, in matters of government no less than in matters of daily life. There were broad rivers in Maryland as in Virginia, and ships traded from wharf to wharf upon them as in the older colony. There were few villages and many spreading plantations. Virginians might have felt that there was practically little difference between their own colony and Lord Baltimore's, had they not seen Roman Catholics enjoy rights of worship there which were not granted them in Virginia. Virginians were expected to observe the ritual and order of the Church of England. Only in Maryland was there freedom in such matters, and the freedom there made Virginians feel, uneasily, that Maryland was in some unlawful way a Jesuit and papist refuge, which would bear jealous watching. The two colonies might speedily have forgot their differences but for that.

Authorities on the history of Maryland during the seventeenth century. The most trustworthy general authorities are John Leeds Bozman's *History of Maryland* (1632-1660); William Hand Browne's *Maryland : the History of a Palatinate ;* John V. L. McMahon's *An Historical View of the Government of Maryland ;* the first volume of J. A. Doyle's *English Colonies in America ;* William T. Brantly's *English in Maryland, 1632-1691,* in the third volume of Winsor's *Narrative and Critical History of America ;*

THE SWARMING OF THE ENGLISH

Edward D. Neill's *Terra Mariae ;* Bancroft and Hildreth's general histories; and the excellent monographs scattered here and there in the nineteen volumes of the *Johns Hopkins University Studies in Historical and Political Science.*

The more important *original sources* are to be found in the *Maryland Archives,* edited by W. Hand Browne; in the *Fund Publications* of the Maryland Historical Society ; in Bacon's *Laws of Maryland ;* in Peter Force's *Tracts and Other Papers relating to the Colonies in North America ;* in W. Hazard's *Historical Collections, Consisting of State Papers and Other Documents:* and in Stedman and Hutchinson's *Library of American Literature.*

WHILE Maryland was being established, a county palatine, and Virginians accommodated their life and temper to the intrusion, affairs moved with strong tide in New England, and the whole face of the country was changed for the English, the Indians, and the Dutch alike. During the ten years 1630–1640, the first ten years after Mr. Winthrop's company came to Boston, a great and ever-increasing immigration poured steadily in at the Bay. These were the years during which there was no Parliament in England, the years during which the government at home seemed most intolerable, and the Puritan colonies in America most inviting, to all Englishmen who took their politics and their religion seriously. No fewer than twenty thousand people came within that single decade to seek homes in New England. In 1634 fourteen ships came in at the Bay with settlers in the single month of June, and the next summer eleven came in in a single day. In 1638 three thousand immigrants arrived within a space of three months. There could be no pause in events while such a tide was running.

Most of the new-comers found the Bay settlements altogether to their liking, and made their homes there very contentedly. They did not object to the strictness of the church government set up by the masterful rulers of the Massachusetts towns, for they were themselves

ARRIVAL OF WINTHROP'S COMPANY IN BOSTON HARBOR

Puritans almost to a man, and liked very well to see their own opinions made compulsory. It did not incommode them that the sterner ministers of the settlements made bold to imitate his Grace of Canterbury and silence those who differed with them. It was an age "when every sect demanded tolerance, yet none had the generosity to grant it," and it was very comfortable to dwell with your own sect.

There was a great deal besides the church in New England,—a great deal to make the novel life in the wilderness stirring and interesting, and worth taking part in. The government, it was true, tried to regulate everything, just as the government at home did: made laws as to what wages should be paid to laborers, what prices should be charged by the merchants; prescribed what uses the farmer should make of his corn, how the fisheries should be conducted, and the fur trade with the Indians carried on. But it was not so easy to enforce such regulations as it was to make them. Fishermen fished in the open sea, upon a long coast, where there were few magistrates; fur traders carried on their barter with the Indians in the depths of the forest; merchants quietly took whatever purchasers were willing to pay; farmers used their land as they thought most profitable and advantageous; and the simple life of the colony was freer than life in England, after all.

There was not a little uneasiness and disquiet, nevertheless. These stirring, austere, uncompromising Puritans, who had crossed the sea to live in a wilderness rather than submit to Laud and the King, were not likely to be all of one mind, or always submissive to one another when they differed; and within less than five years after Mr. Winthrop's first company had established themselves at the Bay signs of a partial breaking up began to appear. Each town was a sort of little commonwealth, and every town followed its minister, if he was of the mettle to lead. Some came from one quarter of the old land which had bred them all, some from another, some from quiet hamlets or rustic country-sides, some from busy towns; and each group, choosing its own place of neighborhood and settlement, kept its own flavor of local habit. And not the flavor of local habit only, but its own favorite views, also, it might be, upon questions of doctrine and polity, or its own strong preferences as to liberty of worship. Congregations had and kept their several characters; the politics of the growing commonwealth sprang out of their differences; and their ministers were their politicians. The Reverend Thomas Hooker, of Newtown, and the Reverend John Cotton, of Boston, were, in those first days, the most notable men among all the ministers of the colonies. Laud had picked both of them out as heretics specially to be feared and disciplined; they had been obliged to make their escape very secretly from England, and had been welcomed at the Bay with a special satisfaction and distinction of greeting upon their landing, in 1633. They were both scholars, and both orators whom it moved men to hear; but they were of opposite views and unlike tempers in dealing with affairs. It was observed after Mr. Hooker was settled at Newtown "that many of the freemen grew very jealous of their liberties." The men of Watertown, near by, ventured to protest very strongly against being taxed for a fort to be built at Newtown, notwith-standing it was meant to serve in case of need against a common enemy; and it was not doubted that Mr. Hooker's very liberal opinions in matters of govern-ment had spread to them, and inclined them thus to press their independence. He was very downright, very formidable in debate; Newtown was contesting with Boston the right to be considered the capital and centre of the Bay settlements; the freemen of the lesser towns looked to it for leadership, and found Mr. Hooker clear in counsel and fit to lead.

Mr. Cotton's views were much more to the liking of the magistrates. "Democracy," he said, "I do not conceive that God ever did ordain as a fit government either for church or commonwealth. If the people be governors, who shall be governed?" He had, more-over, "such an insinuating and melting way in his preaching that he would usually carry his very ad-versary captive,"—a man less rugged than Mr. Hooker, more fitted to charm, the mystical power of a poet and the winning force of an ardent evangelist set forth for all to see in his fine eyes, his ruddy countenance, his locks of chestnut brown, his carriage as of a man sure of his mission and of his mastery. The magistrates generally invited him to preach, accordingly, at every crisis in affairs, to the freemen or to the courts which were to decide what to do, and he had presently such an ascendency "that whatever he delivered in the pulpit was soon put into an order of court or set up as a prac-tice in the church." The Newtown people, who deemed Mr. Hooker no less a master of wise speech and sound doctrine than Mr. Cotton, and Mr. Haynes, their chief citizen, as worthy to be governor as Mr. Winthrop

J Cotton

JOHN COTTON

himself, or Mr. Dudley, one or the other of whom the freemen seemed determined always to choose, grew jealous of a government which seemed to lie so entirely with Boston. They found the combined government of church and company itself a little burdensome. The water, too, at their wharves was too shallow, the soil on their fields too thin, and they were straitened for lack of meadow. Interest, pride, and opinion were very subtly compounded in their disquietude, and neither soft words nor harsh could rid them of it.

They were too loyal and too prudent to wish to disturb the peace and order of the colony by insisting too strenuously or too hastily upon having their own way; but they did not dissemble their discontent, and asked leave of the company's government to remove to another place of settlement. There was not a little alarm and opposition when it was learned that they wished actually to go outside the Massachusetts grant and establish themselves entirely apart on the distant Connecticut. But it became evident very soon that their spirits were too strongly bent upon their new purpose to be restored to ease or contentment where they were. Moreover, the same desire to get away began to show itself elsewhere,—in Watertown and Roxbury and Dorchester; and, with great bodies of new settlers constantly coming in, there seemed no conclusive reason why they should be held, unwilling, within the colony. Though the matter had to be fought through long debates and many delays, therefore, the magistrates at last felt themselves constrained to grant Newtown's petition; and the people of Watertown, Roxbury, and Dorchester chose to consider themselves included in the permission. The three years 1635-1637 saw a notable migration begin. By the spring of 1637 there were fully eight hundred settlers on the banks of the Connecticut and on the shores of the Sound below.

Dutch seamen had discovered the Connecticut so long ago as 1614, when the Virginia Company was still young, and the Massachusetts colony not yet thought of. They had explored also the shores of the Sound below, and both river and Sound had seen their trading boats pass often to and fro these many years. The Dutch had seen the English multiplying fast at

Plymouth and the Bay of Massachusetts; had realized that they must be quick to secure what they had discovered and meant to claim; had formally purchased a tract of land from the Indians at the mid-course of the Connecticut; and at last, just before the English came, had built a little fort there to mark their possession, placing it at the fine turn of the river to which, as it fell out, Mr. Hooker also and his congregation from

MINOT HOUSE, DORCHESTER

Newtown were presently to take a fancy. The Dutch agent in charge had hardly got further in his first work there than the throwing up of an earthen redoubt or two and the planting of a couple of small guns, and had but just named his post "Good Hope" (1633), when the English began to come. Men from Plymouth came first, to build a trading post, and then there followed these congregations from the Bay, as careless of the rights of the Plymouth men as of the rights of the Dutch.

When once their coming had begun they crowded in faster and faster, closer and closer, despite every protest. Not many years went by before they were ploughing the very piece of land upon which the little Dutch fort stood, saying that it was a shame to let good bottom soil lie idle.

Governor Winthrop had sent word to Van Twiller, the Dutch commander at Fort Amsterdam, that he must not build upon the Connecticut. It lay, he said, within the territories of the King of England. But Van Twiller had replied that he held the lands upon the

SIGNATURE OF WOUTER VAN TWILLER

river by as good a title, in the name of the States General of Holland and the authorized West India Company. "In this part of the world are divers heathen lands that are empty of inhabitants," he had pleaded, "so that of a little part or portion thereof there need not be any question." The tide of English immigrants swept in, nevertheless: a few from Plymouth, a great many from the Bay. The Dutch blustered and threatened and protested; but they did nothing more, and were soon outnumbered and surrounded. "These people give it out," reported a Dutch sea-captain returned from the river, "that they are Israelites, and that we at our colony are Egyptians." They called their own countrymen in Virginia the same. It was their mission to set up Puritan commonwealths. Those who were not of their faith and order of living were but a better kind of heathen whom they hoped either to oust or to keep at a safe distance.

In 1635 settlers from Watertown began to build upon the river, six miles below the Dutch at Good Hope, at a place which they presently called Wethersfield. The same year Dorchester people came and sat themselves down beside the little group of protesting Plymouth men at Windsor. There were men in England as well as at the Bay who had cast their eyes upon the valley of the Connecticut as a place to be desired, and they also chose this time to make ready for planting a colony. Lord Say and Sele, Lord Brooke, and others, men of consequence, friends and correspondents of the gentlemen at the Bay, had obtained a grant of lands upon the lower Connecticut and upon the shores of the Sound, as far east as the river of the Narragansetts and as far west as they chose, so long ago as 1631, from the Earl of Warwick, President of the Council for New England; and chose this very time of the migration from the Bay to make their claim good. In 1635 they sent out John Winthrop the younger, the Bay governor's genial and capable son, as governor in their name "of the River Connecticut with the places adjoining," and close upon his heels sent Lieutenant Lion Gardiner, a stout soldier bred to war, like so many another, in the service of the Low Countries, to build fortifications which should make them sure of whatever Mr. Winthrop might occupy. Mr. Winthrop made no serious trouble for the new settlers already come from the Bay. The action of their lordships his employers was friendly, not hostile; his own temper was easy and accommodating; Lieutenant Gardiner was detained at Boston a little while to assist with his expert advice at the construction of fortifications on Fort Hill, ere he went on to the Connecticut; and the fort which he built at the river's mouth when at last he went forward on his errand, though stout enough to guard the place against all comers, was used only to keep the Dutch off. That very year, 1636, Mr. Hooker came with a hundred settlers from Newtown and joined

DUTCH FORT—"GOOD HOPE"

some pioneers who had gone before him and planted themselves, as most unwelcome neighbors, close alongside the Dutch at Good Hope, calling their settlement Hartford.

It had been no easy matter to struggle through the dense tangle of the almost pathless forests all the long ninety miles which lay between these new regions and the Bay. There were household goods and stores to be carried; there were cattle to be fed and driven all the long way; there were women and children to be thought of and spared; and those who made the hard journey spent weeks of weary travelling and lonely camping in those vast forests, which seemed to spread everywhere without border or any limit at all. Even boats could not be expected to make the journey round about by sea unless they chose their season; for when winter came the river was apt to be choked with ice. But these Puritans were not men to be daunted, as the Dutch found to their cost. The journey was made again and again and again, by party after party, as if there were no obstacles which even the women need dread.

Uneasy congregations were not the only people to quit the Bay in that day of eager movement, when men came by the thousands out of England; and the Connecticut was not the only goal of the new emigration. Many a man, many a family who found the rule of the Massachusetts magistrates over irksome, turned their eyes southward and went the shorter journey, of but a little more than forty miles, which carried them through Plymouth's grant of lands into the country of the Narragansetts beyond, where deep rivers and a spreading bay, dotted with inviting islands, made an open way to the sheltered seas of the great Sound below. These shores and islands soon became a place of refuge for all who were specially thrust out from the Bay settlements for errors of life or opinion, and for all who voluntarily quit the austere churches there in search of an absolute individual freedom, such as was not to be had even with Mr. Hooker on the Connecticut. Roger Williams had led the way thither in 1636, the year Mr. Hooker went to Hartford. Mr. Williams was a man whom his very enemies were constrained to love, when they had hearts under their jackets,—even while they

sincerely condemned his opinions. He had come to
the Bay almost as soon as Mr. Winthrop himself, in
February, 1631, in a ship which put in weather-beaten
amidst a great drift of ice; and, though a mere youth,
had given the magistrates trouble from the first. He
was only the son of a merchant tailor of London; but
nature had bestowed upon him gifts of mind and tongue
which put him in a way to succeed as he pleased. He
had become protégé and friend of the great Lord Coke,
had got his training at Cambridge, and then had turned
his back on all "gains and preferments in universities,
city, country, and court," for the sake of absolute liberty
of conscience and belief. He would no more accept
what he did not believe at the Bay than in England. He
upbraided the congregations there which had not openly
separated from the Church of England; he denied the
validity of the colony's charter, saying that the Indians
alone, and not the King, owned and could grant the
land; and he declared that magistrates had no rightful
power except over a man's body and goods, and were
wrong when they tried to command what men should
believe and how they should worship.

The magistrates at the Bay could not permit such
views as these to be preached and keep their authority.
Mr. Williams had a most tender and outspoken conscience upon all things, and was often enough a mere
"haberdasher of small questions," as Mr. Cotton said in
tart jest; but he raised great questions, too, and his rea-
soning as often as not struck at the very foundations of
the curious structure of government the Puritan magistrates had been at such pains to rear. They were in
effect separatists, if you but looked at them from the
other side of the water; and yet they did not suffer their

A

PLATFORM OF
CHURCH DISCIPLINE

GATHERED OUT OF THE WORD OF GOD:
AND AGREED UPON BY THE ELDERS:
AND MESSENGERS OF THE CHURCHES
ASSEMBLED IN THE SYNOD AT CAMBRIDGE
IN NEW ENGLAND

To be prefented to the Churches and Generall Court
for their confideration and acceptance,
in the Lord.

The Eight Moneth Anno **1649**

Pfal: 84 1.   *How amiable are thy Tabernacles O Lord of Hofts?*
Pfal: 26 8.   *Lord I have loved the habitation of thy houfe & the*
place where thine honour dwelleth.
Pfal: 27 ·4.   *One thing have I defired of the Lord that will I feek*
after, that I may dwell in the houfe of the Lord all the
days of my life to behold the Beauty of the Lord & to
inquire in his Temple.

Printed by S G at *Cambridge* in *New England*
and are to be fold at *Cambridge* and *Boston*
Anno Dom: **1·6·4·9·**

TITLE-PAGE OF THE CAMBRIDGE PLATFORM

several churches and congregations to select or maintain what doctrines and practices they pleased. Synods ruled opinion, magistrates enforced their conclusions and their discipline, and Mr. Cotton, set high in the Boston pulpit where the chief men of the government were his disciples and parishioners, was a sort of bishop and primate of the churches. The masters of the Bay had no mind to let Mr. Williams speak or teach as he pleased. And yet it was five years before they made up their minds that he must be expelled from the colony. He was so gentle, so sweet-tempered, so ready to reason calmly with those who differed with him, so awkward to worst in an argument, so passionately loved by all his friends, so mildly hated by most of his foes, that they hesitated again and again what to do. It was unquestionable, nevertheless, that he kept the minds of the Salem people, to whom he preached, in something very like an attitude of rebellion towards the governing authorities of the colony; and at last he was driven out, obliged to fly secretly, even, lest they should seize and send him back to England. Undoubtedly he bred discord and contention wherever he went. He had lived for two years at Plymouth, to escape persecution at the Bay, before the final breach came; and even there, where they were inclined to be almost as liberal as he in matters of opinion, he had made trouble. "A man godly and zealous," the kindly Bradford had pronounced him, "having many precious gifts, but very unsettled in judgment." And so he became a fugitive, and went with four devoted companions, in the midst of bitter winter weather, deep into the icy forests to the southward, to find covert for a sensitive conscience beyond the grants of the crown.

And then, almost immediately, he was able to do the men who had banished him an inestimable service. That very summer (1637) war came,—war with the bold and dangerous Pequots, the Indian masters of the Con-

UNCAS AND HIS SQUAW.   THEIR MARKS

necticut and the shores of the Sound; and nobody but Roger Williams could have held the Narragansett tribes off from joining them to destroy the settlements. A hostile union and concerted onset of all the tribes, effected then, as the Pequots plotted, might have meant annihilation.   There were but five thousand English-men, even yet, scattered in the settlements, and such a rising put everything at stake.   The Narragansetts occupied the lands which lay between Plymouth and the valley of the Connecticut.   Mr. Williams had been much among them while he lived at Plymouth; had learned their language, and thoroughly won their liking.

Their keen and watchful eyes had seen how true and frank and steadfast he was, and how sincere a friend. They had given him lands very gladly when he came among them a fugitive; and now they hearkened to him rather than to the fierce Pequot chiefs, whom he faced at the risk of his life at their very council fires. The magistrates of the Bay had begged his interven-

1637

MIANTONOMO. HIS MARK

tion, and he had undertaken it cheerfully. Such was the generous nature of the man.

The Pequots had grown very hot against the English crowding in. No Englishman's life was safe anywhere, upon the river or the Sound, because of them through the anxious winter of 1636-1637. Men at Lieutenant Gardiner's little fort at Saybrook hardly dared venture forth for fuel or forage. When summer came, therefore, the settlers set themselves ruthlessly to exterminate the tribe. A single bloody season of fire and the sword, and the work was done: the braves of the tribe were slain or driven forth in little despairing groups to the far Hudson in the west; the few women who survived were taken and made slaves of. The terrible business cleared all the river valley and all the nearer regions by the Sound, and English settlers began to pour in again with a new heart.

Massachusetts had lent her aid to the annihilation of the tribe, but the Connecticut towns had begun the deadly work unaided. Until then Massachusetts had maintained a formal oversight, an unbroken assumption of authority among them; but now (1637), being clearly outside the Massachusetts grant, they took leave to hold a General Court of their own and assume independent powers. They had, indeed, no grant themselves, either of land or of authority, from the crown; but there were no King's officers there in the quiet wilderness, and they would not, for the present at any rate, be molested. For two years (1637-1639) they acted without even formal agreement among themselves regarding the method or organization of their government, choosing and obeying their magistrates, electing and holding their assemblies, according to their habit before they came. But in 1639 they adopted a formal constitution, which they called their "Fundamental Orders." Mr. Hooker's liberal temper showed itself very plainly in the principles by which they resolved to be governed. "The foundation of authority is laid in the free consent of the people," he had said, preaching to them from Deuteronomy, i. 13 ("Take you wise men, and understanding, and known among your tribes, and I will make them rulers over you"); and it is best that it should be so, for "by a free choice the hearts of the people will be more ready to yield" obedience. This was the principle of the Fundamental Orders. Their governor was always to be a member of some approved congregation; but any man might be a freeman and voter and fill any other magistracy whose town admitted him to be a resident, without test of doctrine or church membership; and the freemen were to elect the deputies by whom the laws of the colony were to be made in General Court.

The churches at the Bay had found very promptly that they could ill spare Mr. Hooker from their counsels. They had sent for him, indeed, at a very critical juncture

ST. BOTOLPH'S CHURCH, BOSTON, LINCOLNSHIRE, ENGLAND

in 1637: when the ministers needed all the support they could get against a single masterful woman in Boston. Mrs. Anne Hutchinson had come to the colony in 1634, to be near Mr. Cotton once more, whom she had been used to hear and love in old Boston, in Lincolnshire, where, until Laud drove him from the kingdom, he had been minister of stately St. Botolph's. At first she had seemed only a very energetic and helpful woman,

SIR HENRY VANE

with an engaging earnestness and eloquence which gave her a noticeable pre-eminence among her sex in the little town; but before two years were out she had set the whole colony agog. She undertook to

ANNE HUTCHINSON PREACHING IN HER HOUSE IN BOSTON

preach in her own house, and before her day of exile came both men and women were crowding in to hear her. Great and small alike felt the woman's singular charm and power. The whole colony knew before long how many persons of parts and wit had become her partisans,—how many magistrates, gentlemen, scholars, soldiers. Even grave Mr. Winthrop, though he heartily disliked her doctrine, shielded her from criticism. Young Mr. Harry Vane, the most distinguished and engaging youth that had yet come to the colony, whom all had loved from the moment of his landing, and whom the freemen had chosen governor within six months of his coming, though he was but twenty-four, was openly of her party. But only Boston, after all, was within reach of her power. Elsewhere men knew only her opinions; and they were rank heresy. She taught mystical errors touching the Holy Ghost which no church of the colony could accept. She even claimed, it was said, direct revelation to herself. The council to which Mr. Hooker was summoned roundly condemned her opinions. It had hardly done so before it began to look as if the woman's partisans would bring not only ineradicable mischief into the churches, but also disorder and contempt of authority into civil affairs. Boston men who were of her party refused to enlist for the Pequot war. That year, accordingly (1637), saw very peremptory action taken. Mrs. Hutchinson was commanded to quit the colony by the next spring. She turned, in her exile, like other refugees for opinion's sake, to the Narragansett country, whither Roger Williams had shown the way.

And then, the Pequots being driven from the forests, and Massachusetts purged of Mrs. Hutchinson's heresies,

every one began to think again of the new settlements
to the westward and southward, on the Connecticut
and the Sound. The tide of immigrants from over
sea was still pouring in at the Bay, with no show of
slackening. More came in 1638 than ever before.
Finding the lands by the Bay already full, hundreds
pressed on to the farther shores below. Settlements
were presently to be found scattered at intervals, long

OLD FORT AT SAYBROOK, 1639

and short, all the way from Saybrook at the mouth
of the Connecticut to Greenwich, built within twenty
miles of the Dutch at New Amsterdam: here a group
of villages, there an isolated hamlet, set far apart. The
Sound itself was crossed, and new settlements nestled
here and there within the bays and harbors of the northern shore of Long Island. It was plain enough by what
long and steady strides the English were approaching
the gates of the Hudson. New Amsterdam grew and
throve well enough in a slow way; but new colonists

did not come to the Dutch by families, shiploads, congregations, as they came to the Bay. The Dutch saw very clearly what they were to expect. They had already found the English of "so proud a nature that they thought everything belonged to them," and knew very well how aggressive they would be.

Most of the settlements near the river or the Sound, no matter how deeply buried in the forested wilderness,

HOOKER'S HOUSE AT HARTFORD

connected themselves with the free and simple government set up by Mr. Hooker's people at Hartford; but no community or government owned the region more than another, and some chose to keep an independent authority of their own. In June, 1637, a very notable company had arrived at the Bay under the leadership of the Reverend John Davenport,—people of substance, merchants for the more part, the chief men of a congregation Mr. Davenport had served in London. They wished, above all things else, to keep together, make and maintain a separate church and parish for Mr. Davenport, and live their life in a place of settlement

John Davenport   JOHN DAVENPORT

of their own. They found what they wanted (1638) within a safe and pleasing harbor on the Sound, which they presently called New Haven. Busy Captain de Vries, putting in at New Haven in June, 1639, found "already three hundred houses and a handsome church" built there. They had been at the pains to erect "fair and stately houses, wherein they at first outdid the rest of the country"; and they soon found their town become a sort of capital for that part of the shore. Almost immediately other settlements sprang up close at hand,—Milford upon the one hand, Guilford on the other, and others still as the years went by. Deeming themselves a group apart, though in the midst of towns joined with the river settlements above them, these associated themselves with Mr. Davenport's people to form an independent government, upon another model. No one but a church member, admitted under

HOUSE AT GUILFORD, 1639

the strictest tests of belief, could among them, it was decreed, either vote or hold office. They tried, in their singular stiffness and candor of faith in an absolute and uncompromising Puritan order, for commonwealth no less than for church, to make the laws of the Old Testament the laws of their own political life and practice also, and steadfastly held themselves to the self-denying liberty they had left the Old World to find.

Settlements grew almost as numerously in the Narragansett country, though not in just the same way. By 1638 some fifty settlers had drawn about Mr. Williams at the place of refuge which he had reverently called "Providence"; and as the other shores of the Sound filled, Narragansett Bay was not overlooked. Colonists crossed the waters of the Bay from Providence, which lay at its head, to the fair island at its seaward end, which the Dutch had named Rhode (Red) Island, because when first they saw it its cliffs showed ruddy in the sun. There Pocasset and Newport were founded. But the settlers on those waters were not like settlers elsewhere. They were people of many creeds and beliefs,—Baptists, dissentient Puritans, partisans of Mrs. Hutchinson,—men and women whose views and practices were not tolerated elsewhere. They came hither, as Mr. Williams had come, to escape being governed at all in matters of opinion. Mr. Williams had spoken, in his catholic tolerance, of "the people of God wheresoever scattered about Babel's banks either in Rome or England." It looked for a little as if the shores of Narragansett were to be the banks of Babel. Men of all creeds made free to establish themselves upon them. They set up very simple forms of government, —for they generally agreed in wishing as little government of any kind as possible,—and yet, how slack soever the authority of rulers among them, they did not find it easy to live together. They were often turbulent; always disposed, upon a disagreement, to break away and live elsewhere in small, independent groups, rather than in strictly organized communities. Mrs. Hutchinson herself, who came to Pocasset when forced to leave the Bay in 1638, did not stay long. Her presence bred disquiet even there, and she soon removed again (1642) to a place on Long Island, within the territory of the Dutch, only twelve miles from New Amsterdam.

Many of the immigrants who crowded the ships that came yearly in at the Bay came expressly to be with old friends and comrades at Plymouth; and not a few others turned thither also when they had had time to make a choice. Until 1632, which was twelve years after its founding, the single village upon the hill at Plymouth had sufficed to hold all who came; but between 1632 and 1639 the colony was transformed by mere growth. Seven towns were after that to be counted within the Plymouth grant; the government of the colony had been readjusted, and a new code of laws drawn up. A new and more various life had come to the quiet bay. Captain Standish had been the first to set the example of expansion. In 1632 he had crossed the little harbor which lay before the town and had begun to build at Duxbury. Others followed his lead. Villages sprang up in quick succession, both on the shore to the northward facing the open sea, and on the shore to the southward which lay within the sheltering curve of the great arm of Cape Cod. Settlers turned inland also, and began to build at Taunton, full twenty miles and more away in the forest, upon one of the larger streams which ran southward into the bay of Narragansett.

The Dutch were not slow to see what they must do against the swarming of the English at their doors. The best and only chance for New Netherland, it was plain, lay in pushing her own enterprises very vigorously and multiplying her own population as fast as possible, and so growing too strong to be despised and encroached upon. The great grants of land and privilege offered to patroons had attracted a few rich purchasers, but not many actual settlers. Not many could be found who wished to go to the New World to live under feudal lords more absolute than any in the Old. The company changed its policy, therefore. It offered patroons

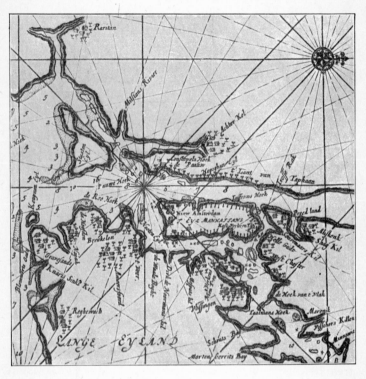

MAP OF NEW AMSTERDAM AND VICINITY, 1666

less and actual farmers more. It arranged to let every settler have land "according to his condition and means," and to give him free passage to the colony; and it opened the trade of the colony to all upon equal terms. French Huguenots, as well as Dutch farmers, even

Englishmen from New England and Virginia, came to take advantage of the new terms of settlement. It was no small part of the attraction of the place for the English in New England that there was as complete liberty of conscience in New Netherland as at Providence with Mr. Williams or on Rhode Island. The colony grew steadily, therefore, and in a way to countenance very sanguine hopes.

But every prospect was marred by bad administration. The place was spoiled by a veritable pest of governors. The company sent out either mere clerks, or else men of questionable reputation and ruined fortunes, to take charge of its affairs. The weak and sluggish Van Twiller, who blustered and threatened but did not act when the English began to crowd in at the Connecticut, was succeeded in 1638 by the no less foolish Kieft,—a good enough agent for business to be done on a small scale and by rote, but incapable of understanding strong and efficient men or any large question of policy; and Kieft brought everything to the verge of utter ruin by his faithless and exasperating dealings with the Indians. He prompted attacks upon them for what they had not done; demanded tribute from friendly tribes who were the colony's best defence against those which were hostile; suffered them to be treacherously massacred when they fled to Fort Amsterdam for succor against the Iroquois; finally brought friend and foe alike to such a pitch of exasperation that they united for a war of extermination. Every outlying farm was rendered uninhabitable; scores of white men were put to death; the nearer English settlements suffered with the Dutch, and all the slow work of peaceful growth was undone. In that fearful year of plunder and death (1643) Anne Hutchinson lost her life, her last refuge swept away with the rest.

In the South River the very friends of the Dutch played them false. Kieft did not scruple, in 1642, to drive away a body of English settlers there whom the New Haven people had sent down to take the trade of the region; but quite three years before that other rivals had fixed themselves on the western banks of the river of whom it was not so easy to get rid. In 1638 Samuel Blomaert, who had but a little while before taken out the rights of a patroon under the Dutch West India Company, and Peter Minuit, who had once been the

SIGNATURE OF SAMUEL BLOMAERT

company's governor at New Amsterdam, set up a colony at the South River under a charter from the King of Sweden, Minuit himself leading the settlers thither, and bringing with him more Dutch than Swedes. And there the colony he established remained, safe at its "Fort Christina," because stronger than the Dutch at their lonely "Fort Nassau." The new-comers cheerfully lent a hand in driving the New Haven men out; but they kept their own foothold; multiplied faster than the men of New Netherland; grew steadily Swedish rather than Dutch in blood; and seemed likely, though neighborly enough for the present, to oust their lagging rivals in good season.

The principal *general authorities* on the history of New England during the seventeenth century are John Gorham Palfrey's *His-*

tory of New England (1492–1774) and *Compendious History of New England* (1497–1765); the second and third volumes of J. A. Doyle's *English Colonies in America*; John Fiske's *Beginnings of New England*; Justin Winsor's *Narrative and Critical History of America,* volumes III. and V.; Bancroft and Hildreth's general histories of the country.

The development of the several colonies which were added to Massachusetts in the Puritan group, and some of the special phases of the growth of the little New England commonwealths, may be traced in detail in Benjamin Trumbull's *Complete History of Connecticut, from 1630 to 1764;* Samuel Greene Arnold's *History of Rhode Island;* George W. Greene's *Short History of Rhode Island;* Edward E. Atwater's *History of the Colony of New Haven to its Absorption into Connecticut;* Charles H. Levermore's *The Republic of New Haven* (one of the *Johns Hopkins Studies*); Hubbard's *History of Massachusetts* in the *Collections* of the Massachusetts Historical Society; Peter Oliver's *The Puritan Commonwealth: An Historical View of the Puritan Government in Massachusetts;* Charles Francis Adams's *Three Episodes of Massachusetts History;* various monographs in the *Johns Hopkins Studies in Historical and Political Science;* and W. B. Weeden's *Economic and Social History of New England.*

The chief *original sources* are to be found in the *Colonial Records* of Rhode Island, Connecticut, and New Haven; the *Provincial and Town Papers of New Hampshire;* the *Massachusetts Colony Records;* the *Collections* of the Historical Societies of Massachusetts, Connecticut, New Hampshire, and Maine; Farmer and Moore's *Historical Collections of New Hampshire;* the publications of the Gorges Society; the *Narragansett Club Publications;* Peter Force's *Tracts and Other Papers Relating to the Colonies in North America;* the *Publications* of the Prince Society; John Winthrop's *History of Massachusetts,* edited by J. Savage, and *The Life and Letters of John Winthrop,* edited by R. C. Winthrop; and Thomas Hutchinson's *History of Massachusetts.*

On the 19th of May, 1643, commissioners representing Massachusetts, Plymouth, Connecticut, and New Haven, sitting in Boston, made a formal agreement that their colonies should be joined in a confederation for mutual support and defence, under the name of The United Colonies of New England. Mr. Hooker and Mr. Haynes had been urging such a union for quite six years, ever since the synod of churches had sat, in 1637, to draw up its list of heresies and unwholesome opinions in reproof of Mrs. Hutchinson and her supporters in Boston; for the Connecticut towns had no charter of their own, and these prudent gentlemen knew how much they might need the aid and countenance of their neighbor colonies should the time come when their rights were too narrowly questioned,—by the Dutch, for example. New Haven, with her government but just formed, and with as little show of charter rights from the crown as the towns of the Connecticut, was glad to come into the arrangement for very much the same reason. Plymouth and Massachusetts agreed because there was common danger from the Indians all about them and from the French in the north, and because there were awkward boundary disputes to be settled between the several colonies, for whose discussion and peaceful decision it would be well to have some common authority like that of a confederation. Massachusetts,

STATUE OF SIR HENRY VANE

by far the greatest and strongest of the colonies, no doubt expected to rule in its counsels. The other colonies hoped to restrain Massachusetts and hold her back from dominating overmuch.

That same year, 1643, Roger Williams went to England to get a charter for the settlements in the Narragansett country. It was hard to deny Mr. Williams anything he seriously set himself to get and went in person to obtain, and young Mr. Vane, who had been governor of Massachusetts in Mrs. Hutchinson's day, and who was Mr. Williams's friend, being now returned into England, was one of the "Commissioners for Plantations" whom the Parliament in England had recently appointed to govern the colonies; so that by March, 1644, "Rhode Island and Providence Plantations" had their own separate charter rights, and could assert them upon a footing of equality with Plymouth and Massachusetts. The settlements on the Narragansett waters had been excluded from the confederation formed in Boston because they were thought to be too full of troublesome persons and uneasy politicians to be safe or peaceful partners; but now that they had their own charter they could endure the exclusion without too much anxiety as to how their rights should fare.

The articles of confederation which gave the Puritan colonies their new union spoke of advice and protection expected from the mother country over sea; but they said nothing of England's authority over her colonies. The contracting parties conducted themselves like independent states, and asked no one's leave to unite. At another time, perhaps, they would have hesitated; but now they had an opportunity that might not come again. England was convulsed with civil war. At last she was reckoning with Charles, the false king, who for ten years had refused to summon a Parliament, and who had seemed from year to year to become more

CHARLES I.

and more openly an enemy of the liberties which Englishmen most cherished, until the slow fire of indignation against him, which had smouldered hotter and hotter the dark years through, burst into flame in Scotland, and men saw a revolution at hand. Even Charles saw then how fierce a tempest had sprung up against him, and yielded so far as to consent to call a Parliament. The Parliament, once called together, assumed a novel tone of mastery. Under the leadership of such men as the steadfast Pym, direct in speech, indomitable in purpose, no revolutionist, but a man whom it was wise for a king who ignored the laws to fear, and Hampden, whom all just men loved because he was so gentle and gracious in his gallant uprightness, the Commons impeached the men who had aided the King's injustice, and proceeded to bring the government back again under the ancient restraints of freedom.

Charles saw that he must either yield all or else openly resist. He chose to resist; set up his royal standard at Nottingham (August, 1642); called upon all loyal subjects to rally about it for the defence of their king; and so brought civil war and a revolution upon England. Every one knows what followed: how at first the cause of the Parliament seemed desperate, because Pym died and Hampden was slain, and there was no leader in the field who could withstand Prince Rupert; and then how an increasing number of steadfast partisans of Parliament in Norfolk, Cambridge, Essex, Suffolk, and Hertford formed an association, levied troops, and put Oliver Cromwell beside the Duke of Manchester to command them; how Cromwell's horsemen drove Prince Rupert's men in hopeless, utter rout from Marston Moor on a July day in 1644; and then, in June of the next year, at Naseby, repeated the terrible work, and finished what they had begun, to the utter undoing of the King; and how Charles, on a day in May, 1646, seeing his cause desperate, surrendered himself into the hands

174

of the Scots, in order to play the game of politics,—the game of war having failed; knowing that the Scots, who were Presbyterians, would not easily come to terms with Cromwell, whom it would be very hard to bring into any Presbyterian arrangement.

Three years went by, and the subtile King lay dead upon the scaffold at Whitehall (January, 1649), showing

VIEW OF NEW AMSTERDAM, 1656

a gentle majesty and steadfastness at the last, though he had not known how to keep faith even with himself and his own friends while he lived. He was not brought to his death by the Parliament, but by the army, and the army did not represent the nation. Cromwell had not put his men to any test of opinion; but in the end it had turned out that the rank and file of the army were, for the time at any rate, "Independents," holding opinions concerning worship and the government of church and state like those which he held, and the strict

Puritans who had gone over sea into New England. They were the more likely to hold their opinions stiffly and without compromise because Parliament, leagued with the leading men of Scotland, was Presbyterian, was jealous of the army's rising power, and wished to disband and send them home without so much as voting their pay. Though Cromwell held them back as long as

WATER GATE, FOOT OF WALL STREET, NEW YORK, 1674

he could from violent measures, they at last made bold to win by force in their contest with the Commons, and he found it best to lead them. All who were not partisans of the army and of the Independents were driven from the House, and the handful who remained brought the King to his trial and condemnation, and finally to his death at Whitehall, close by the window of his banqueting hall. They were acting for a minority of the nation, but no one dared withstand them.

With such matters as these to look upon at home,

FIRST MEETING-HOUSE, 1634–1638.   ROGER WILLIAMS'S CHURCH

there was no time in England to watch events in the far colonies across the sea. The New Englanders could form their confederation if they pleased without molestation. But if the war gave them freedom of action, it brought other things in its train which were not so acceptable. No new settlers came any more. Men began to return into England instead,—ministers to give counsel, as well as soldiers and men of affairs to lend their aid in the field of action. Stephen Winthrop, the governor's son, George Fenwick, of Saybrook, Israel Stoughton, captain of the Massachusetts men sent against the Pequots, and not a few others of general note, entered the Parliamentary army. Edward Hopkins, who had but just finished his term as governor of Connecticut, and Edward Winslow, who had been with the Plymouth people from the first, went back into England to assist in the administration of the navy maintained against the King. Mr. Hooker was begged by letters signed by many chief men of the Parliament to come over and lend his counsel in the task of reforming the Church, but would not go because he saw the Presbyterians so strong in Parliament, and did not wish to be in a minority. It looked for a little as if John Winthrop himself might be drawn into the struggle at home. Mr. Hugh Peter, of Salem, who had been a leader among those who drove Roger Williams forth from the Bay into the wilderness, was among the first despatched to England to give counsel in the

SIGNATURE OF ROGER WILLIAMS

Puritan cause; and it was he who "preached the funeral sermon to the King, after sentence, out of Esaias": "Thou art cast out of the grave like an abominable branch, . . . as a carcass trodden under feet. . . . Because thou hast destroyed thy land and slain thy people." It was a Puritan revolution, and the thoughts and hopes of the Puritans in New England turned eagerly towards the mother country again.

It was a very serious thing for the Puritan colonies that their rapid growth was thus stopped of a sudden. It meant that no farmer there could any longer get the high prices for his cattle or for his corn, or for any crop he might raise, which he had learned to count on while immigrants poured in; that the value of land suddenly declined; that every trade fell off; that money, always exceedingly scarce from the first, now stopped

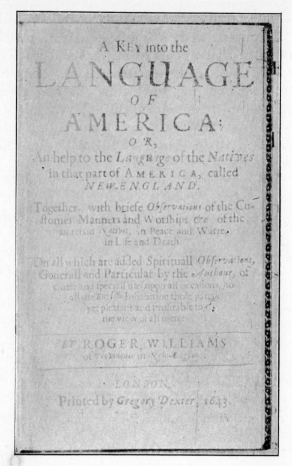

A KEY into the
LANGUAGE
OF
AMERICA:
OR,
An help to the *Language* of the *Natives*
in that part of AMERICA, called
NEW-ENGLAND.

Together with briefe *Observations* of the Customes, Manners and Worships, &c. of the
aforesaid *Natives*, in Peace and Warre,
in Life and Death.

On all which are added Spirituall *Observations*,
Generall and Particular by the *Authour*, of
chiefe and speciall use (upon all occasions,) to
all the *English* Inhabiting those parts;
yet pleasant and profitable to
the view of all men:

BY ROGER WILLIAMS
of Providence in New-England.

LONDON,
Printed by *Gregory Dexter*, 1643.

TITLE-PAGE OF ROGER WILLIAMS'S "LANGUAGE OF AMERICA"

coming in altogether, for it could come only from England. Some of the colonists lost heart, and hastened
to return to England, not to see the wars, but to escape
ruin. Some took themselves off to the islands of the
West Indies, where, they heard, it was easy to live.
Some joined the Dutch at Hudson's River. It required

not a little steadiness of mind and purpose, not a little painful economy and watchful good management, to get over the shock of such changes and settle down to make the best of the new conditions. Happily the colonists were not men to be dismayed, and had made too good a beginning to fear actual failure. Massachusetts, with her four counties and thirty towns, her fourteen hundred freemen, her organized militia, her educated

THE CANAL, BROAD STREET, NEW YORK, 1659

clergy, and her established leadership among the colonies of the north, was ready to stand upon her own feet, with a little practice; and the other colonies, on the Connecticut and on the Sound, had proved themselves from the first to be fit to live by struggle. Massachusetts had even established a college of her own, and was no longer entirely dependent upon the universities at home to supply her clergymen and her gentlefolk with an education. The General Court had begun the setting up of a proper school in 1636, had changed the name of Newtown, where the school was placed, to Cambridge, in order that it might seem to the ear a more suitable home for it, and, two years later, had called the little college Harvard, in honor of the young clergyman who, dying in their midst (1638), had bequeathed to it his library of two hundred and sixty books, and a few hundred pounds, the half of his modest estate. The doughty little commonwealth had already learned in no small degree how to be sufficient unto herself.

Only Virginia reaped any sort of direct material benefit from the civil wars. Her people were not Puritans. They were drawn from the general body of Englishmen who believed in the sanctity of the Church and of the crown, at the same time that they loved their own liberty and did not mean to be imposed upon by any man's power, whether in church or state. Perhaps they did not know how much they were attached to the established order of things in England until those days. of revolution came; for until then they had been very easy-going in church discipline, and very tolerant indeed of differences of opinion, acting untrammelled and without too much thought of uniformity, as if in the spirit of the free wilderness about them; for they were men picked out of every rank and class, followed no one opinion, lived in separated houses, and looked every one chiefly to his own business. But when they heard of what was happening over sea in England they knew their own minds very promptly, for they looked upon disloyalty as a thing not to be separated from dishonor. Their assembly, when they learned of the King's death, flatly declared it an act of treason, the more impudent because brought about under the forms of law, and

FARRER'S MAP OF VIRGINIA 1651

resolved that it was the right of Charles, the dead monarch's son, to be king in Virginia "and all other of his Majesty's dominions and countries." They were led in their hot defiance by their governor, Sir William Berkeley, who had come to them by the King's appointment the very year Charles set up his standard at Nottingham (1642). A bluff, outspoken man was Sir William, bringing with him to the rural colony the gallant, thoroughbred airs of the court, and standing square to his opinions and traditions. But the frank and genial humor of his ordinary moods gave place to very hot and stubborn passion when he saw how things went against the King at home, and it was he who led the Burgesses in their defiant protests against the revolution.

The King's partisans in England, when they found things grow too desperate for them at home, were quick to perceive that Virginia was their natural and safest place of refuge, and her open countries began slowly to fill with exiled Cavaliers. The tide-water counties began to get a new character with this fresh infusion of rich blood, and Virginia grew while New England stood still.

But it was not safe for Virginia, for all she was so far away, to defy the Puritan government at home. For, the fighting in England over, and the intrigue that centred about the King ended, the Puritan leaders were masters of the kingdom. Even Sir William Berkeley swallowed his mortification and submitted when an armed frigate came into the river (1652) with commissioners on board whose orders were to reduce Virginia to obedience to the commonwealth, and who had the promise of all necessary force to sustain them in what

they did. The real temper of the colony was not as
fierce as the tones of the Burgesses' resolutions had been
when they condemned those who had killed the King.
There was a singular mixture among the Virginians

JOHN HAMPDEN

of loyal sentiment and stubborn, matter-of-fact independence in all practical matters. The rank and file
of them, though Church of England men in religion,
had in them a dash of hard-headed sagacity very like

the circumspect caution of the Puritans themselves,—a way of seeing the wrong time to fight and the right time to make terms. They saw as well as other men the necessity to bow, at any rate for the present, to a government which had Cromwell at the head of its forces, —and Sir William Berkeley accepted the course of prudence with the rest. The commissioners, fortunately, were men who knew the colony, and they came with instructions which prescribed in a very generous spirit what they should do. It had been one of the first acts

SIGNATURE OF SIR WILLIAM BERKELEY

of the Long Parliament to grant again to "the Adventurers and Planters in Virginia" the old charter rights which James had annulled, and to permit the old Virginia patent to be taken out again under the broad seal of England; and its commissioners were instructed accordingly. They did not oblige Virginia to receive a governor at the hands of the Parliament; they simply ousted the King's men, and put the government into the hands of the Burgesses, the people's representatives. Until 1660 Virginia was to rule herself, practically as she pleased, herself a commonwealth, subject to the greater commonwealth over sea.

She was very well able to take care of herself. Her neighborly counties held already more than fifteen thousand thrifty English people,—and more, a great many, were being added now that ships were fast coming in full of the fugitive friends of the King,—sixteen hundred, once and again, in a single company. Twenty thousand cattle grazed upon the broad pastures which sloped green to the margins of the rivers, as well as great flocks of sheep, and, in the deep woods, swine without number. Ships passed constantly in and out at the rivers,—from Boston and New Amsterdam, as well as from London and Bristol, and the home ports of Holland. Though many in the colony ate from rich plate and were wealthy, the well-to-do were not much better off than the humble, after all, for no man needed to be very poor where there was such abundance for all. It was a democratic place enough, and the poor man's small beer went down with as keen a relish as the rich man's wine. The rough, disorderly ways of the early days of settlement were past, and were beginning to be forgotten now. Virginia had acquired some of the sober dignity and quiet of a settled common-wealth. Her clergy had often, at first, been as rough fellows as those not of the cloth, who came to Virginia to have leave to live as they pleased, and had been no help to religion; but now men of a better sort began to rule in her churches, and to sweeten her life with true piety. She could fare very well upon her own resources, whether in church or state. The Parliament's com-missioners had made rules under which any reasonable man could live. Any who pleased might drink the King's health within doors, at their own boards, if they did nothing against authority out-of-doors. Speech was not to be throttled, men's sentiments were not to be too curiously looked into. The exiled royalists who came steadily in, seeking a refuge, need sacrifice nothing but what they had already given up. Their very flight was confession of defeat; here in Virginia

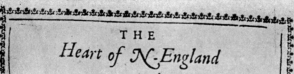

THE
Heart of N-England
rent at the
BLASPHEMIES
OF THE PRESENT
GENERATION.

Or

A brief Tractate concerning the Doctrine of
the Quakers, Demonstrating the destructive nature
thereof, to Religion, the Churches, and the State,
with consideration of the Remedy against it.
Occasional Satisfaction to Objections, and Confir-
mation of the contrary Trueth.

By *JOHN NORTON*, Teacher of the
Church of Christ at *Boston*.
Who was appointed thereunto by the Order of the
GENERAL COURT.

I know thy works, and thy labour, and patience,
and how thou canst not bear them which are evill;
and thou hast tryed them which say they are Apostles,
and are not, and hast found them lyars Rev: 2. 2.

Printed by *Samuel Green*, at CAMBRIDG
in *New-England*. 1 6 5 9.

TITLE-PAGE OF NORTON'S BOOK AGAINST THE QUAKERS

defeat might seem less bitter, though the necessity to obey Parliament and the Lord Protector was not less imperative.

In Maryland, Virginia's neighbor, things wore a much harder face because of the revolution. The Parliament's commissioners were friends of Virginia, and had dealt very lightly with her, but they felt no kindness for Maryland. Before their coming the little province had had its own taste of war. Late in 1644 William Clayborne, seeing his opportunity, had seized Kent Island again, from which Lord Baltimore had driven him at the first setting up of his government; and in February, 1645, one Richard Ingle, master of the armed ship *Reformation*, bearing letters of marque from the Parliament, put men and arms ashore and seized St. Mary's itself. The *Reformation* was one of eight ships the Parliament had commissioned to bring food, clothes, arms, and ammunition to the province "for the supply and defence and relief" of the planters who were of its party against the King; and those who bore the commission used their power with little scruple. Master Ingle, in particular, had the strong stomach for adventure and for his own gain which comes to roving sailors in a lawless age, and a spirit of mastery which was his own. Ships out of Bristol carried the King's commission to take ships out of London; ships out of London the authority of the Parliament to take all craft out of Bristol, and every man acted for his party and himself. "It pleased God," Ingle said, "to enable him to take divers places" from the papists and malignants, "and to make him a support to the well affected"; and it was close upon two years before Leonard Calvert found himself strong enough to bring a force out of

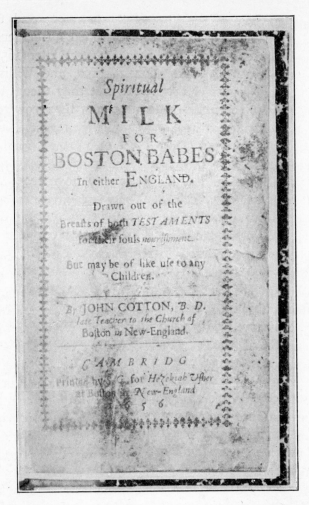

Spiritual

MILK

FOR

BOSTON BABES

In either ENGLAND.

Drawn out of the
Breasts of both TESTAMENTS
for their souls nourishment.

But may be of like use to any
Children.

By JOHN COTTON, B. D.
late Teacher to the Church of
Boston in New-England.

CAMBRIDG
Printed by S. G. for Hezekiah Usher
at Boston in New-England
5 6

TITLE-PAGE OF ONE OF JOHN COTTON'S TREATISES

Virginia and re-establish his brother's authority. The
government of the province had not been destroyed, the
while, but there had been a sad time of disorder and
reprisal; partisans of the proprietor and of the King

had seen their affairs shamefully handled; and the men who ruled had governed as if upon an exigency in a day of revolution. And then, six years later (1652), the parliamentary commissioners came, and William Clayborne was one of them. At first they thought it best to make the same moderate use of their power in Maryland that they had made of it in Virginia, and simply confirmed its government as it stood, content that it should be conducted in the name of the Commonwealth in England; but they thought themselves warranted in keeping their authority under their commission from the Parliament, and two years later asserted it again to effect a revolution, because they saw the proprietor likely to regain control of his province. They assisted (1654) to put the government of the colony into the hands of a group of Puritans who had made a settlement there, and for a time,—until Cromwell himself intervened to give Lord Baltimore his rights again,—the distracted province was ruled very rigorously by a masterful minority.

The Puritans who were thus made masters had most of them come out of Virginia. For a little while they had maintained their congregations unmolested, almost unnoticed, in Virginia, in the quiet lower counties below the river and near the Bay; but Berkeley had driven them out when he grew hot against the Puritan revolutionists in England, and they had made a new home for themselves in tolerant Maryland, where not only custom, but a formal Act of Toleration, drawn by the proprietor's own hand, made them safe against molestation. They did not use their own power gently, however, when the parliamentary commissioners gave them control of the government of the colony; and called to-

FACSIMILE OF CROMWELL'S LETTER TO JOHN COTTON

Worthy Sr and my Christian freind/ I receaued yours, a few dayes si=
thence, it was welcom to mee, be=
cause signed by you, whome I loue
and Honour in the Lord. but moued
to see the same grounds of our alliances some of our
shewinge in you, that haue in us.
to quiet us to our worke, and sup=
port us therein, w:ch hath had grea=
test difficultyd in our engagemdnt
in Scotland; by reason wee haue had
to dod. w:th some, whoo weare (f verily
thinke) Goodly, but thorough weaknesse,
and the Subtillys of Sathan, inuolued
in interests, against the Lord. and
his people. w:th what tendernesse wee
haue proceeded w:th such, and that
in syncerityd, our papers (w:ch f
suppose you haue seen) well in part
manifest, and I giue you some com=
fortable assurance off. The Lord
hath maruelously appeared euen

against them: and now agame
when all the power was devolved
into the Scottish kinge and the
malignant pactie, they innadeing
England, the Lord ~~braine~~ rayned
upon them such snares as the
enclosed will shew, ~~bequerime~~ only
the narrahive is short in this,
that of there whole armie where
the Narrahive was feamed not
fine of there whole Armie
wend returned. Surely Sr the
Lord is quratly to ber feared,
as to ber praissed. wer need yr
~~pple~~ prayers in this as much as
ever, how shall wee behave
oure selves aftor such mercyes?
what is the Lord a doeinge?
what prophesies are now full-
fillinge? whoe is a God like ours?

to knowe his will, to doe his will
are both of him.

I tooke this libertye from busi-
nesse to salute you: this in a
word, truly I am readye to serve
you, and the rest of our brethren
and the churches with you. I am
a poore weake creature, and not
worthye the name of a worme,
yett accepted to serve
and his people indeed

freind betweene you.
you knowe not mee, my
inordinatenesse
nesse, my passions, my weak-
fullnesse, and every way unfitt-
nesse to my worke, yett, yett,
the Lord whoe will have mer-
cye on whome Her will, does
as you see. pray for mee, salute
all christian freindes though un=
knowen, I rest
                    your affectionate freind,
Octobr 25: 1651   to serve you O Cromwell

gether an assembly of their partisans to support them. They repealed the Act of Toleration, and no more suffered any man to differ with them than Laud had permitted Englishmen at home to differ with him before the revolution, or than the Puritan Parliament had tolerated dissent from its purposes since. For three years they had their own way in all things, and the province was no better off for their handling when the courts in England at last gave it back into Lord Baltimore's hands, in 1657.

The new government in England meant to maintain its authority in the colonies and at home no less steadily and effectively than the old government of the King had done, and Cromwell, when he became Lord Protector, proved a more watchful master than Charles had ever been, as well as a more just. But Massachusetts took leave, because it was a government of Puritans and her own friends, to practise a little more openly the independence in the management of her own affairs which she had all along meant and contrived to maintain. She very promptly dropped the oath of allegiance to the King when she heard that the Parliament had broken with him (1643); and now, when a commission which the Parliament itself had set up sought to dictate to her, though it had explicit authority "to provide for, order, and dispose all things as it saw fit" in the management of the colonies, she boldly declared that she thought it her right to govern herself without interference or appeal, so long as she remained obedient and faithful to the government at home in all things that affected Englishmen everywhere.

She took occasion, while things went their new way, to set her own government in order (1644),—between

Mr. Pym's death and the day of Marston Moor,—while England was too much distracted to know what sort of government she herself had. The Bay government was not a comfortable government for any man to live under

JOHN PYM

who was not a Puritan. The magistrates stood behind the ministers of the congregation to enforce their judgments in matters of morals, as well as to fulfil the law's commands in every ordinary matter of government. The discipline of life which was thus imposed upon all alike, of whatever age or estate, made the little commonwealth a model place of steady work and clean living. Nowhere else in the world would you hear so few oaths uttered, or see so few idle or drunk or begging. The magistrates watched the lives and behavior of their people very diligently, and no man who did not live decently and reverently could long escape their punishment or rebuke. The weak and the sensitive suffered

PETER STUYVESANT'S BOWERY HOUSE

very keenly under their rigor, and those who were naturally gay and of high spirits found it very irksome and painful to be always on their guard not to jest too often or amuse themselves overmuch. Sometimes the reason of a high-wrought nature here and there would break down under the burden of stern doctrine and colorless living put upon it by church and state. But the strong and naturally grave men who predominated in the staid towns found it a fine tonic to be so governed, and were confirmed in their strength and self-control. In 1648 they drew more sharply than ever the lines of the church's right to rule, in a formal platform adopted, in synod, at Cambridge. The authority of the clergy was given clear definition of law; the power of the magistrates to coerce all churches which should "walk incorrigibly or obstinately in any corrupt way of their own," was affirmed more definitely than ever; and the ecclesiastical polity of the New England churches was declared to be such a "Congregational" establishment as should in no wise be confounded with any of "those corrupt sects and heresies which showed themselves under the vast title of Independency." This "Cambridge platform" the General Court submitted to the congregations and the several congregations adopted. Henceforth no man need doubt what compulsion of worship and belief he must live under there.

New Haven and Connecticut could have admired the orderly peace and prosperity of Massachusetts more if they had found her juster and more generous in the part she played in the government of the confederation. In that they deemed her selfish. The colonies had an equal vote in the council of the confederation, but were obliged by the articles of their union to contribute to its expenses, not equally, but in proportion to their population, which threw much the heaviest burden upon Massachusetts. She, therefore, opposed all occasion of expense in matters in which she was not herself particularly interested. She would not vote to help New Haven get redress for the injuries which the Dutch had done her in the South River; she absolutely refused to take part in levying war on the Dutch when the other commissioners of the confederation voted it, when England

Nevv-Haven's

Settling in

NEW-ENGLAND.

AND SOME

LAWES

FOR

GOVERNMENT:

Publifhed for the Ufe of that Colony.

Though fome of the Orders intended for
prefent convenience, may probably
be hereafter altered, and as
need requireth other
Lawes added.

LONDON:

Printed by *M.S.* for *Livewell Chapman*, at the
Crowne in *Popes-head-* Alley.
1 6 5 6.

TITLE-PAGE OF THE EARLIEST BOOK ON THE NEW HAVEN COLONY

herself was at war with the Netherlands; and she demanded tolls upon all goods brought from the other colonies into Boston, because the confederation sustained Connecticut's right to charge tolls at the mouth of the Connecticut River. It seemed a profitless partnership enough to Plymouth and Connecticut, but most of all to New Haven, which had suffered most from the Dutch.

The New Haven men were merchants, and had not forgot their purposes of trade when they came from London with Mr. Davenport to seek a place where they might worship as they pleased. They had chosen the quiet southerly harbor at which they had settled because of its outlook upon regions of trade, north and south, within the forests and along the coasts which spread about them; and it had come close upon ruining them to lose all that they had laid out upon the settlement on the South River of New Netherland which the Dutch had destroyed. Nothing seemed to prosper with them. While they yet waited and hoped to get redress from the Dutch, they laid out a full thousand pounds upon the fittings and freight of a vessel to be sent into England, with some of their chief men on board, to obtain both trade and a charter in the mother country; and had cut the ice in their harbor at midwinter in their haste to get her out. But they never saw the ship again, nor any that went out upon her. One June day, indeed, in 1649, while a vague mist lay upon the bay, there suddenly appeared the form of a ship upon the water, with all her tackling, and her sails set, "and presently after, upon the top of the poop, a man standing with one arm akimbo under his left side, and in his right hand a sword stretched out towards the sea.

ARRIVAL OF STUYVESANT AT NEW AMSTERDAM

Then from the side of the ship which was from the town arose a great smoke. which covered all the ship, and in that smoke she vanished away." For as much as a quarter of an hour the crowd upon the beach, both men and women, gazed steadfast upon the phantom; and many deemed when it was gone that they had seen their lost craft and treasure. That same year, 1649, they turned again to the commissioners of the confederation with their urgent prayer for forcible redress against the Dutch,—and got nothing. Massachusetts again declined to lend her assistance, and war between England and Holland blew off before it came to actual conflict between the Dutch and the English in America. New Netherland began to show itself stronger than ever under a new governor,—no very wise man, but much better than Van Twiller and Kieft and the rest of the foolish men who had preceded him.

Peter Stuyvesant had been sent over as governor in 1647. He made an odd figure with his wooden leg, marvellously contrived with bands and ornaments of silver, and the sly burghers of the simple-mannered New World made a jest of his pretentious way of carrying himself by calling him their "grand Muscovy Duke." But he moved about among them with a certain show of force and dignity, for all that, if he did have to limp at the business, and he made men understand at least that he was a person to be obeyed. He was quite as truculent and violent of temper and arbitrary as Kieft had been before him; but he was much more efficient, and was able to come to an understanding with his neighbors, both on the Sound and within the South River. In 1650 a treaty was at last agreed upon with the English which fixed the boundaries between their settlements and the Dutch, reserving on the Connecticut itself only the fort of Good Hope and the little plot of ground about it; and though the people at Hartford

PETER STUYVESANT

nevertheless seized and appropriated that also, once for all, when they heard of the war between the Netherlands and the Commonwealth at home (1654), that was no great loss, and did not disturb the boundaries which had been drawn beyond Greenwich on the mainland and athwart Long Island at Oyster Bay. Stuyvesant more than compensated himself for the loss of Good Hope; for that same year (1654) he took a force that could not be withstood to the South River, and conclusively put an end to the Swedish power there, making the river once more a part of New Netherland, not to be disputed again by Sweden.

OLD STATE HOUSE OF NEW AMSTERDAM

Death the while thrust his hand into the affairs of New England, and sadly shifted the parts men were to play there. In 1647, the year Stuyvesant came, Mr. Hooker had been taken, leaving no such shrewd and kindly statesman and pastor behind him; and in 1649, the year the King died upon the scaffold, John Winthrop departed,—the man who had founded Massachusetts, and who had seemed its stay and prop. Then Mr. Cotton died (1652), to be followed, scarcely six months later, by Mr. Dudley. Mr. Haynes went in 1654, and

ORIGINAL TOWN HOUSE, BOSTON, 1657–1711. BUILT BY THOMAS JOY, FROM HIS OWN DESIGN

the gentle Winslow in 1655; and then Standish, the bluff soldier, who had carried so many of Plymouth's burdens at the first (1656), and Bradford, the peasant gentleman and scholar, whom all had loved and trusted (1657). Last of all, Mr. Eaton was taken (1658), and New Haven mourned her grave and princely merchant and governor as one whom she could not replace. The first generation of leaders had passed away; men of a new kind were to take their places.

Endecott still lived, to be elected governor year after year till he died (1665). Thirty years in the wilderness had done little to soften his hard rigor against those who offended, though it were never so little, against the law or order of the colony, whether in matters of life or doctrine. He was quick to bring men and women alike to punishment for slight offences; and the days of his rule were darkened by the execution of several Quakers who had refused to quit the colony when bidden. The air cleared a little of such distempers when he was gone.

The *authorities* and *sources* for the period covered in this Section have already been named, in connection with the history of the several colonies, under Sections I. to V. of this chapter. There should be added, however, to the authorities on *Virginia*, Robert Beverley's *History of Virginia*, which is here almost a first-hand source.

For the history of this period in England the exhaustive authority is Mr. Samuel Rawson Gardiner, in his *History of the Great Civil War, 1642-1649*, and his *History of the Commonwealth and Protectorate*.

VII. THE RESTORATION

ALL Europe feared England's power while Cromwell ruled. No such masterful spirit had stood at the front of her affairs since great Elizabeth's day, and there seemed to be revived in him the same wide vision in the making of plans and the same passionate resoluteness in executing them that had drawn Ralegh and Drake and Frobisher and Hawkins forth to their adventures on the sea, seeking conquests for England at the ends of the earth. It was not enough for him that he should subdue Ireland and quiet Scotland by force of arms, and make himself master at home. He deemed it his duty to lead England forward once again towards the great destiny of conquest and power which men had had clear sight of in the brave days of Shakespeare and good Queen Bess, but had seemed to forget and lose heart for while the unkingly Stuarts reigned. Acting upon secret instructions from the Protector, Major Robert Sedgwick, of Charlestown, in Massachusetts, and Captain John Leverett, of Boston, led an English force into Acadia, where the French were, upon the Bay of Fundy, and made it by sudden conquest an English province (1654). That same year Admiral Blake was sent into the Mediterranean to punish the Duke of Tuscany and the pirates of Tunis for injuries they had inflicted on merchantmen out of England; and the next year, 1655, a great fleet was put upon the seas to go into the West Indies against the possessions of Spain, and there gave the great island of Jamaica the flag and commerce of England.

Cromwell had demanded of Spain freedom of trade in the West Indies and the exemption of English subjects from the horrid tyranny of the Inquisition; not because he thought that Spain would grant these things, but because he saw what England must demand and get if she would compete for power with the Spaniard, who still every year drew great stores of gold and silver

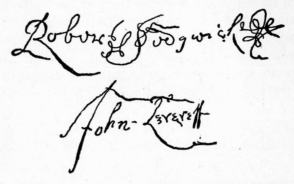

SIGNATURES OF ROBERT SEDGWICK AND JOHN LEVERETT

and other treasure from her rich colonies in the West. He no doubt expected Spain to refuse what he demanded, and meant from the first to send men-of-war to take what she would not give. He seemed to know, like the statesman he was, what the possession of America and of her trade would mean in the future, and he was acting under counsel from America itself in what he did: the counsel of Mr. Hooke, the shrewd pastor at New Haven, his confidant and relative, of Mr. Cotton, of Boston, whom Mr. Hooke had urged to write to the Lord Protector, and of Roger Williams, who was in England (1651–

1654) while the thing was being considered, who was often admitted to private conferences with the Lord Protector, and whose knowledge, sagacity, frankness, and sweetness of nature proved much to that great soldier's liking. These men were Puritans of the same stock, breeding, and party with himself. They hated Spain as he did, as the chief instrument of the Romish Church, and they wished to cut her treasures off.

The Lord Protector was no stranger to America. It was told that he had himself tried to get away to the safe refuge of the Puritan colonies in the dark days when Charles was master and would not call a Parliament. He had joined others in signing the letter which certain members of Parliament sent into New England inviting Mr. Hooker to come back to England to assist at the reform of the Church; and he had been one of the commissioners whom Parliament had appointed in 1643 to dispose of all things in the colonies as they saw fit—the commissioners from whom Mr. Williams had obtained his charter for the Providence Plantations. No doubt Cromwell would have made a greater empire for England in America had his hands been free at home; but death overtook him ere his plans had widened to that great work (3 September, 1658).

Massachusetts used the time while the Commonwealth stood not only to settle a little more carefully the forms of her own government, but also to extend her jurisdiction over the new settlements which were springing up about her to the northward, and to set up a mint of her own to coin shillings, sixpences, and threepences to take the place of the money so fast drawn off into England to pay for the goods brought thence. And, since her people were nearly all of one mind and creed in

A DECLARATION

Of the SAD and GREAT

Perſecution and Martyrdom

Of the People of God, called
QUAKERS, in *NEW-ENGLAND*,
for the Worſhipping of God.

22 have been Baniſhed upon pain of Death,
03 have been MARTYRED.
03 have had their Right-Ears cut.
01 hath been burned in the Hand with the letter H.
31 Perſons have received 650 Stripes.
01 was beat while his Body was like a jelly.
Several were beat with Pitched Ropes.
Five Appeals made to *England*, were denied
by the Rulers of *Boſton*.
One thouſand forty four pounds worth of Goods hath
been taken from them (being poor men) for meeting
together in the fear of the Lord, and for keeping the
Commands of Chriſt.
One now lyeth in Iron-fetters, condemned to dye.

ALSO:

Some CONSIDERATIONS, preſented to the KING, which is
in *Anſwer* to a Petition and Addreſs, which was preſented
unto Him by the General Court at *Boſton*: Subſcribed by
I. *Endicot*, the chief Perſecutor there; thinking thereby to
cover themſelves from the Blood of the Innocent.

*Gal. 4. 29. But as then, he that was born after the fleſh, perſecuted
him that was born after the Spirit, even ſo it is now.*

God hath no reſpect to *Cains Sacrifice*, that killed his Brother about Religion.

London, Printed for *Robert Wilſon*, in *Martins Le Grand*,

TITLE-PAGE OF PROTEST OF THE QUAKERS, PUBLISHED IN LONDON
EARLY IN 1660

matters of religion, she took occasion to regulate her
church affairs even more stringently than the Puritans
at home ventured to regulate the faith and worship
of England. She put her new "Cambridge platform"
rigorously into practice, stopping to doubt neither its
righteousness nor its expediency. She not only thrust
Quakers out, but sternly forbade all dissent from the
doctrines taught by her preachers, and required that
even the officers of her militia should be members of the
authorized church. There was here no radical change.
Massachusetts was but confirming herself in her old
ways with a somewhat freer hand than before, because
no fear of reproof or correction from the government
over sea any longer restrained her.

Virginia, meanwhile, underwent a veritable trans-
formation. When the Parlia-
mentary commissioners came
to Jamestown in 1652, in their
frigate, to summon the colony
to make her submission to
the Commonwealth, they had
had to deal, as they knew,
with no special class of Englishmen like the Puritans in
New England, but with average Englishmen, mixed of
gentle and common, too far
away from England to be very
hot party men upon either side

SEAL OF VIRGINIA AFTER THE
RESTORATION

in respect of the sad quarrel between the King and the
Puritans. They professed, like other English subjects,
to belong to the Church of England, and their own government there in the colony had but the other day sent

nearly a thousand settlers packing out of its jurisdiction into Maryland because, though quiet people enough and fair to deal with in other matters, they had refused to observe the forms of the Church, and had openly prac- tised a manner of worship and of church government like that set up in New England, and now in England itself. But the Virginians, take them rank and file, were not really very strenuous about the matter them- selves. The Burgesses commanded very strictly the ob- servance of the canons of the Church of England in every matter of worship; but the scattered congregations of easy-going colonists were in fact very lax, and ob- served them only so far as was convenient and to their taste. Archbishop Laud would very likely have thought them little better than Puritans in the way they governed their churches,—for each neighborhood of planters was left to choose its own minister and to go its own way in the regulation of its forms of service. They revered the great mother Church over sea very sincerely, and meant to be faithful to it in everything that should seem es- sential; but the free life of the New World made them very democratic in the ordering of the details of practice, and they were glad that there were no bishops nearer than England. Some among them, perhaps not a few scattered here and there, were known to think like the Puritans in matters of government, if not in matters of worship; and there were men of substance among the number, men like Captain Samuel Mathews, for ex- ample, one of the chief men of means in the colony, whom all deemed "a true lover of Virginia," notwithstanding the frank and open freedom he used in differing with his neighbors when they exalted Church or King.

Captain Richard Bennett they elected governor under

JAMES BLAIR

the new agreement with the Commonwealth in England, notwithstanding the fact that he had been the leader of the Puritans whom Sir William Berkeley had driven into Maryland for contumacy in disobeying the laws of the colony, and had, besides, been one of the commissioners who had compelled them to submit to the Puritan government in England. When his term was out they chose Mr. Edward Digges, who was no Puritan, and then Captain Mathews himself, who died in the office just as the Commonwealth came to an end in England. The Burgesses were the real governors of the colony all the while, as they made Captain Bennett and Mr. Digges and Captain Mathews understand, and the House of Burgesses was made up of men of all opinions. Some parts of the colony were very impatient under the government that had ousted the King, and those parts were as freely represented among the Burgesses as any others. There was Northampton county, for example, lying almost by itself, on the "eastern shore" beyond the Bay, whose local authorities, not content with what the Burgesses had put into their resolutions concerning the death of the King, had themselves proclaimed Charles, the dead king's son, "King of England, Scotland, Ireland, and Virginia, and all other remote provinces and colonies, New England, and the Caribda Islands" (December, 1649). It cost a good deal of watchfulness and steadiness in governing to keep such men quiet even under their own assembly; and the Burgesses themselves hastened to call Sir William Berkeley back to the governorship again when they learned that Richard Cromwell had declined to maintain his father's place in the government at home. England had not yet enthroned Charles II.; things hung for many months in a doubtful balance; and the Burgesses conducted Virginia's government the while in their own name. Sir William Berkeley was only

Charles   CHARLES II.

their servant as yet, and they chose Captain Bennett also to be of the governor's council; but Sir William was more to their mind, after all, than commonwealth men, and they very promptly acknowledged him the King's governor again when they knew that Charles had been received and restored in England,—returning with a certain sense of relief to their old allegiance and their long accustomed ways of government.

Then it was that it began to become apparent how much Virginia had changed while the Commonwealth stood, and how uneasy she must have become had the Commonwealth lasted much longer. During that time a great host of royalist refugees had sought her out as a place of shelter and safety, if not of freedom,—a great company, to be counted at first by the hundreds and then by the thousands, until Virginia seemed altered almost in her very nature and make-up. The steady tide of immigration did not stop even at the fall of the Commonwealth and the restoration of Charles, the King. The congenial province still continued to draw to itself many a Cavalier family whom days of disaster and revolution had unsettled, or to whom she now seemed a natural place of enterprise and adventure. Not the regions of the first settlement merely, on either side the James, but the broad tide-water country to the northward also between the York and the Rappahannock, between the Rappahannock and the great Potomac, filled with the crowding new-comers. In 1648 there had been but fifteen thousand English people in Virginia; in 1670 there were thirty-eight thousand, and nine new counties sent Burgesses to her assembly. The population had more than doubled in about twenty years; and most of those who had come from over sea to be added to her own natural increase were Cavaliers, men who wished to see the rightful King upon the throne, and England secure once more under her ancient constitution.

This great immigration, though it brought to Virginia men who were all of one tradition and way of life, did not mean the introduction of a new class of gentle-folk. No doubt a great many of them were of gentle blood and breeding; no doubt an unusual number of them were persons of means, who could afford to purchase and maintain large estates on the rich river bottoms. It is certain that with their coming came also a very noticeable change in the scale and style of living in the colony. More big grants of land were made. Great plantations and expensive establishments became more common than before. Negro slaves were more in request, and the Dutch and New England ships which brought them in from Africa or the Indies more welcome in the Bay than ever. The society of the little province was enriched by the gracious presence of many a courtier, many a cultured gentleman, many a family of elegance and fine breeding, drawn from the very heart of English society. But this was not the first time that Virginia had seen such people come to live on her fertile acres. There was no novelty except in their numbers. There had been men of like extraction, manners, and principles in the colony from the first,—not a great many, perhaps, but quite enough to keep all men in remembrance of the gentle middle and upper classes at home: gentlemen as well as boors, noted blood and obscure, good manners and bad. There now came men a great many like Colonel Richard Lee, of the ancient family of Coton Hall in Shropshire, honored since the thirteenth century with places of trust and distinction in the public service; like Mr. John Washington, grandson of Lawrence Washington, of Sulgrave and Brington, and cousin of that gallant Colonel Henry Washington who upon a famous day had stormed Bristol with Rupert,—who had told Fairfax he would hold Worcester till he should receive his Majesty's command to yield it up, even though his Majesty were already a prisoner; men like the Randolphs, the Pendletons, the Madisons, the Ludwells, the Parkes, the Marshalls, the Cabells, the Carys, who had time out of mind felt the compulsion of honor bred in them by the duties they had performed, the positions they had won, the responsibilities they had proved themselves able to carry. But Virginia received them as of no novel kind or tradition. Men of Cavalier blood were no breeders of novelties. They were not men who had doctrines to preach or new ideals of their own to set up. They were merely the better sort of average Englishmen. They preferred settled ways of life; had more relish for tradition than for risky reforms; professed no taste for innovation, no passion for seeing things made unlike what they had been in older days gone by,—openly preferred the long established order of English life. They gave to the rapidly growing tide-water counties in which they settled their characteristic tastes and social qualities; established a very definite sentiment about government and social relationships, like that at home; but they rather confirmed the old tendencies of the place than gave it a new character.

They only made complete the contrast that had all along in some degree existed between Virginia and New England. It was men of the King's party, the party of the Restoration, to whom Virginia now became a familiar home, and the coming of the second Charles to the throne seemed an event full of cheer in the southern colony. Men bred like the Cavalier families of Virginia in every social matter, drawn from sound county stock and ancient lines time out of mind gentle and elevated to the ranks of honor, had gone into New England also at the first: Winthrops, Dudleys, Winslows, Saltonstalls, Chaunceys,—men bred, like Cromwell himself, to influence and position. But they were men whom a new way of thought had withdrawn from the traditions of their class and set apart to be singular and unlike the rest of Englishmen. To the Cavalier gentlemen of Virginia the home government now seemed healed and sound again, and affairs settled to that old familiar order which best suited Virginia's taste and habit. There came increase of wealth, too, with the tide of immigration, which ran steadily on; and the plantations seemed quick with hopeful life once more. To the Puritan gentlemen of New England, on the contrary, all hopeful reform seemed at an end, and the government they had made and cherished put in critical jeopardy. Their chief concern, now as always, was to be let alone; to be allowed to conduct their affairs for themselves, after the Puritan model, unchecked and unmolested. They had liked the setting up of the Commonwealth in England, not because they felt any passion against the King, but because the new government was a government of their own friends, and might no doubt be counted upon to indulge them in the practice of a complete self-government. Their passion was for independence. Their care was to cut off all appeal from their authority to that of the government at home. They meant to maintain a commonwealth of their own; and there was good reason to fear that the King, whom the Puritans in England had kept from his throne, and Cromwell's death had brought back, would look with little favor upon their pretensions.

As a matter of fact, it was the Puritan Parliament itself

which had taken the first step towards bringing all
the colonies alike into subjection to the government in
England,—at any rate, in everything that affected commerce. In 1651 it had enacted that no merchandise
either of Asia, Africa, or America should be imported
into England, Ireland, or any English colony except
in ships built within the kingdom or its colonies, owned
by British subjects, and navigated by English masters
and English crews,—unless brought directly from the
place of its growth or from the place of its manufacture
in Europe. It was no new policy, but an old, confirmed
and extended to a broader reach and efficacy. It was
not meant as a blow at the trade of the colonies,—except,
it might be, at the trade of Virginia and the Barbadoes,
which had been a little too bold, outspoken, and in-
subordinate in protesting against the execution of
Charles and the setting up of the Commonwealth,—but
for the aggrandizement of Englishmen everywhere. Sir
George Downing had suggested the passage of the
act, a man born in New England and of the Puritan
interest on both sides of the sea. The new leaders
in England had revived the purposes and hopes of
Gilbert and Ralegh and Elizabeth, and meant to build
up a great merchant marine for England, and so make
her the centre of a great naval empire. They were
striking at the Dutch, their rivals in the carrying trade
of the seas, and not at the colonists in America, their
fellow-subjects. The Dutch recognized the act as a
blow in the face, and war promptly ensued, in which
they were worsted and the new mercantile policy was
made secure against them. It was a way of mastery
which caught the spirit of the age, and men of the King's
party liked it as well as those did who had followed

Cromwell. The very first Parliament that met after the Restoration (1660) adopted the same policy with an added stringency. It forbade any man not a subject of the realm to establish himself as a merchant or factor in the colonies, and it explicitly repeated the prohibitions of the act of 1651 with regard to merchandise brought out of America or Asia or Africa. Certain articles, moreover, produced in the colonies, it reserved to be handled exclusively by English merchants in England. Chief among these were the sugar of the Barbadoes and the tobacco of Virginia. These were not only to be carried exclusively in English bottoms, but were also to be exported only to England. It seemed a great hardship to the Virginian planters that they were thus put at a double disadvantage, forbidden to choose their own carriers and also forbidden to choose their own markets, obliged both to pay English freights, whatever they might be, and also to put everything into the hands of English middlemen. But Parliament gave them compensation, after all, and they found in due course that there was little less profit under the acts than before. Treble duties were put upon Spanish tobacco brought into England, that they might have the market to themselves, and a great part of their cargoes went on, through England, to the northern countries of the continent, with a handsome rebate of duties. They soon adjusted themselves to the system.

An act of 1663 made a very weighty addition to the series of restrictions. It forbade the importation into the colonies of "any commodity of the growth, production, or manufacture of Europe" except out of England and in English ships. No ship, though an English ship and manned by English seamen, might thereafter lawfully carry any merchandise directly out of Europe to the colonies. England must be the *entrepôt*. The frank preamble of the act stated its purpose. It was intended to maintain "a greater correspondence and kindness" between the people of his Majesty's plantations and the people of England, to keep the plantations "in a firmer dependence" upon the kingdom, and to render them "yet more beneficial and advantageous unto it" by using them for "the further employment and increase of English shipping and seamen" and as "the vent of English woollen and other manufactures and commodities, rendering the navigation to and from the same cheap and safe, and making this kingdom a staple, not only of the commodities of those plantations, but also of the commodities of other countries and places, for the supplying of them." Such, added the preamble, was "the usage of other nations, to keep their plantations' trades to themselves."

To obey these acts meant to exclude all foreign ships from English ports in America, the ships of the neighborly Dutch at New Amsterdam with the rest, and to cut the colonies off from all direct transactions with foreign markets, making them dependent upon England whether they bought or sold. But, if obedience were forced upon them, there were compensations. English capital, after all, supplied them with the means to grow and to make their adventures in commerce, and deserved its reasonable encouragement without grudging. Ships built in the colonies were English-built ships under the meaning of the statutes, and New England turned her hand with a great aptitude and ardor to building ships out of the incomparable timber which stood everywhere ready in her virgin forests. It transformed both her life and her industry to be thus set to rival the Dutch and the shipbuilders and seamen at home in the carrying trade of the seas, and every village that had its port or outlet set up stocks and built sea-going craft, if only to carry cargoes up and down the long coast. European stuffs, too, though brought out of England, oftentimes cost less than the English themselves had to pay for them; for in England they paid duties to his Majesty's customs, but if they were sent forward to the colonies the duties were remitted. The system appeared not so niggardly when looked at on every side.

Moreover, the acts might be disobeyed with some impunity at the safe distance of America. New England did, in fact, openly ignore them. For more than fifteen years after the passage of the act of 1660 she traded as she pleased, in entire disregard of the authority of Parliament. These Acts of Navigation (for so they were called) had not been passed with their consent, the Massachusetts General Court declared, and were not binding upon them. But neglect of laws passed by Parliament only made it the more certain that the government of the King would some day, when it found leisure for the business, turn its hand to discipline and bring the too independent colonists to a reckoning. The colonies were now no longer the insignificant settlements they had been before the air in England darkened with the trouble between Parliament and Charles I. They had become lusty States, very noticeable, and altogether worthy of the attention of the home government. They were subject, under the arrangements of English law, entirely to the authority of the King in council,—that is, to such members of the King's

Privy Council as he chose to clothe with authority in the matter of their government; and there stood at the elbow of the new King a man of statesmanlike power

Edward Earl of CLARENDON Lord High CHANCELLOR of England. and Chancellor of the University of Oxford An° D̄ni 1667

EDWARD HYDE, EARL OF CLARENDON

and perception, Edward Hyde, Earl of Clarendon, whose advice began to give a novel thoroughness of system to the administration of the growing possessions of the crown. He became a member of the general council appointed to oversee all foreign plantations at the very outset of the new King's reign (December, 1660), and presently became a member also of the special committee of the Privy Council charged in particular with the settlement of the affairs of New England (May, 1661), giving to its policy spirit and direction.

Massachusetts was keenly aware how open she was to attack, if it came to a question of obedience. Her magistrates had from the first systematically neglected to administer the oath of allegiance to new settlers, though their charter explicitly commanded that it should be administered. They administered, instead, an oath of fidelity to the government of Massachusetts. They had excluded members of the Church of England not only from the right to vote, but even from the right to use the appointed services of that Church in their worship. They had extended their authority over districts to the northward which clearly lay beyond the bounds of the lands granted them in their charter. They had denied to those who sought to exercise it the right to appeal from their decisions to the King's courts in England, and had even punished some who made as if they would appeal in spite of them. They were not surprised, therefore, when, in 1664, the King appointed commissioners to look into their dealings with the crown, with their neighbors, and with their own subjects, and prepared themselves for as shrewd a defence and fight for their independent powers as the circumstances might permit. They had offended in the very points in respect of which Clarendon felt most clearly justified in insisting that they should submit to royal authority. He meant to insist upon an observance of the Navigation Acts, upon the recognition of the civil rights of members of the Church of England, and upon the subordination of the colonial courts to the courts of the King by the establishment of the right of appeal, at any rate in cases of special significance.

Massachusetts, moreover, had been very slow about proclaiming Charles II. king. Her magistrates had waited more than a year after first hearing of the Restoration before they publicly and in proper form pro-

THE WALL, WALL STREET, NEW YORK, 1660

claimed his authority, wishing to make sure that the unwelcome news was true and the King actually accepted in England. The ship which brought the news, in August, 1660, had brought also two officers of Cromwell's army, Edward Whalley and William Goffe, who had signed the late King Charles's death-warrant, and were now fugitives from England; for the Parliament had excluded from the Act of Indemnity and pardon, which had accompanied the new King's return, all "regicides," all who had been directly concerned in the death of Charles I. Many of those who had not fled were already under arrest, Sir Harry Vane among the rest, presently to be sent to the scaffold; but the colonists in New England befriended these men who had fled to them, and Colonel John Dixwell also, who soon followed them; and kept them safe against all searches of the King's officers until they died. Massachusetts sent agents of her own into England to make her peace with the King; but they returned with a letter from his Majesty which commanded an immediate recognition of his authority, the administration of justice in his name, the toleration of the Church of England, and a repeal of the laws by which the right to vote was restricted to members of their Puritan churches. It was the sharp tenor of this letter that made them anxious how they should fare at the hands of the royal commissioners who came in 1664.

Fortunately for Massachusetts, the settlement of her government was not the first or chief business of the commissioners. Their titles showed for what they had been chosen,—Colonel Richard Nicolls, Colonel Sir Robert Carr, and Colonel George Cartwright, officers of the royal army, with but one civilian associate, Samuel Maverick, a one-time resident of Massachusetts, but long since forced out of the colony for his failure to agree with the exacting magistrates in matters of worship and of government. Though they were directed "to dispose the people" of the New England settlements "to an active submission and obedience to the King's government," and came upon a business like that which the commissioners of the Commonwealth had twelve years ago so quietly carried through in Virginia and Maryland, their chief errand was to make an end of the Dutch power in America. They came with a fleet of three ships of war and a transport carrying four hundred and fifty soldiers, to capture New Amsterdam and make New Netherland once for all an English province. Not that England was at war with the Dutch. It was claimed that England had from the first owned all the country of the coast, and that the Dutch had all along been

SIGNATURES OF THE COMMISSIONERS TO RETAKE NEW NETHERLAND

intruders, as the English settlers on the Connecticut had again and again told them. The claim was not just; for the Dutch had unquestionably been the first to discover and the first to settle upon the Hudson, the Connecticut, and the great Sound itself; but it was true that the kings of England had all along asserted their exclusive title there, as elsewhere on the long Atlantic seaboard, all the way from the French settlements in the north to Florida and the Spanish settlements in the south, and had more than once included the lands upon which the settlements of New Netherland lay in their grants to trading companies and to individuals who promised to take settlers out.

"The Dutch had enjoyed New Netherland during the distractions of the reign of Charles II. without any other interruption" than the occupation of their lands upon the Connecticut by the New Englanders, and the settlement first of the Swedes and then of the English on the Delaware; but the ministers of Charles II., though they were "for some time perplexed in what light to view them, whether as subjects or as aliens, determined

EARLY WINDMILL, NEW YORK

at length that New Netherland ought in justice to be resumed." Such was the way in which English writers afterwards spoke of the matter, putting into their histories what they wished to believe. But the facts are plain enough. The claim of right was a pretext. English statesmen saw that they could not enforce the Navigation Acts in America so long as the English colonies had the Dutch next door to trade with as they pleased. They saw also that the great Hudson was the natural highway to the heart of the continent and to the land of the fur trade. They knew how inconvenient it was, and how dangerous it might become, to have the Dutch power thrust, a solid wedge, between their own northern and southern colonies, covering the central port and natural mart of the coast. They made up their minds, therefore, to take what they wanted by force. The ministers of Charles were but resuming the plans of Cromwell, who had sent a fleet into America to do this very thing, when the first Navigation Act provoked the Dutch to war, and had withdrawn it only because he immediately got, by a treaty of peace, something that he wanted more.

The first step taken by King Charles was to give New Netherland by royal grant to his brother James, the Duke of York and Albany, all the lands lying within the wide sweep of a line drawn up the western bank of the Connecticut River, from the sources of the Connecticut to the sources of the Hudson, "thence to the head of the Mohawk branch of the Hudson River, and thence to the east side of Delaware Bay" (March, 1664). The commissioners were sent on their men-of-war to take possession in the Duke's name. The thing proved easy enough. The doughty Stuyvesant was taken entirely by surprise, had no force with which to withstand Charles's ships, found the peaceable burghers about him loath to fight, and yielded without a blow struck, though he would rather have lain in his grave, he said, bitterly, than make such a surrender. There was no choice with but an hundred and fifty men trained to arms and but twenty guns upon the fort against the King's frigates and an army.

The settlement of the forms of government under which the English should rule was almost as easily effected; for Colonel Nicolls, the English commander, was not less a statesman than a soldier, knew how to be wisely generous and make liberal provision for privileges and securities of right and property which should belong to the Dutch settlers as freely as to the English, and within a year of his coming had transformed New

SLAB MARKING THE TOMB OF PETER STUYVESANT, OUTER WALL OF
ST. MARK'S CHURCH, NEW YORK

Netherland into New York, under laws which promised toleration and good government, and which all sensible men accepted with satisfaction. And yet it was not, Colonel Nicolls found, an easy place at which to be set down as governor. There was a very puzzling mixture of peoples and of institutions to be dealt with. The Duke's grant covered all of Long Island, which the Dutch had not tried to govern beyond Oyster Bay. English towns dotted the island which had been parts of Connecticut or of the colony of New Haven, and which had always used their English liberty in matters of local government. Near at hand upon the island, and up the long reaches of the North River, where the Dutch towns lay, magistrates ruled whom Stuyvesant had appointed, or the agents of some potent patroon. At New Amsterdam itself men of all nationalities, creeds, and ways of life were to be found mixed in cosmopolitan variety. On the South River were settlements half Swedish, half Dutch. It was impossible to thrust upon all of these a single system of government. Where the Dutch had ruled it was still feasible to govern without elections, through officers whom the governor appointed, and under laws enacted in the governor's council; but the English towns insisted upon having a voice in the choice of their own magistrates, and used their town meetings, whether they were legal or not under the Duke's decrees, to direct the officers whom they elected in the discharge of their duties. Fortunately Colonel Nicolls was but thirty-nine when he came to the task, had still the elasticity of a young man in his make-up, saw with clear, frank eyes, and was no less conciliatory than firm in action. His tact and decision established "the Duke's Laws" with little difficulty outside the English towns, though with many a local adaptation, and even in the English towns he managed to lack nothing that was essential to his authority. The governor and his council, themselves the appointees and servants of the Duke of York, ruled the whole colony without serious let or obstacle, and made new laws when there was need; but ruled with a new temperance which the Dutch had not seen before, and made provision for just methods of administration in everything. There was trial by jury, there were equality and unquestioned security in the tenure of lands, and practically absolute freedom of belief and worship; and the inhabitants of the captured province saw much to be content with.

It was of the first consequence that English power should be well and wisely rooted there at the gates of the Hudson. That mighty river, pouring down out of the north, came straight from the country where the French were masters. Its valley and the valleys which opened into its own, bringing their waters also out of the north, and the lakes which stretched above, almost to the stream of the St. Lawrence, were the veritable keys to the continent. There English power must be kept or broken. Charles, the King, may not have comprehended the full significance of what he did when he sent his fleet to plunder the Dutch and make New Netherland a province for his brother. But every thoughtful man in America knew. Here was not only the greatest of all the highways to the country of the fur trade; here was also the strategic centre of the continent itself. Whoever should be indeed master here might call all America his own, upon all the coast and throughout all the deep forests which lay upon it. The colonies of the English could not be drawn together either for mastery or for defence without this central harbor and water - way to the heart of the north. It was well the Duke had sent so wise a man and so capable to make good the English foothold there.

But it was not a little disturbing that the King had sent the fleet to annex a part of New England as well as all of New Netherland to the Duke's domain. He had made his grant to the Duke run eastward to the banks of the Connecticut; and yet (had he forgotten?)

he had already given away the lands there, on both sides of the river, not two years before, by a formal charter grant (April, 1662), to John Winthrop, governor of the settlements that had taken the name Connecticut. Until then the settlers there had had no charter at all. For seventeen years they had lived under a government of their own framing, and with only such rights as they were able to buy under former grants made by the old Council for New England. But now, by the address and good management of their capable governor, the accomplished son of the John Winthrop who had died governor of Massachusetts, they had been secured in their rights both of occupation and of government under a most liberal charter, which left them as free to choose their own governors as before. The younger Winthrop, himself a man of fifty-six, was well known in England. It was his privilege to assist, almost at this very time, in the foundation of the Royal Society, and afterwards to become one of its Fellows; he had influential friends near the person of the King; his own charm of manner and gifts of mind were calculated to make his Majesty forget that he was son-in-law to Hugh Peter, who had preached to the first Charles at his condemnation; and he got what he wanted for Connecticut.

In the indefinite terms of his charter the boundaries of Connecticut were to run westward to the South Sea (as the English still called the Pacific); to the deep chagrin of the New Haven people, it included their own towns; certainly it ran athwart the later gift to the Duke of York. For the time being that was not a matter of much practical importance. The Duke did not attempt to exercise his authority in the Connecticut settlements, and an agreement was presently reached that Connecticut should have jurisdiction to within twenty miles of the Hudson. Though that agreement never received the royal sanction, it sufficed for the moment. What seemed to the New Haven people of much more consequence was that Governor Winthrop had managed to sweep their towns within his charter grant. They liked neither the politics nor the church government of the Connecticut towns above and about them, and for two years stood out against being absorbed. It seemed better, however, to belong to Connecticut than to belong to the Duke of York's province, as they might be obliged to if they did not accept Mr. Winthrop's charter; Mr. Winthrop was himself very wise, moderate, and patient in pressing the union upon them; and in 1665 they yielded, making Mr. Winthrop governor of the united towns upon the river and the Sound.

The King's commissioners did not fare very well when they turned from the taking of New Netherland to the examination and settlement of affairs in Massachusetts. In the other colonies which they had been directed to set in order they had little difficulty. Connecticut and Rhode Island were just now in favor at court, and gave the commissioners little to do except settle the boundaries between them. Rhode Island had obtained a new charter from the King in July, 1663, scarcely a year after Mr. Winthrop had got his for Connecticut; and, though she had had some difficulty in saving an important strip of territory which Connecticut's charter had been made to include, that matter was in the way to be adjusted before the commissioners came. In Plymouth they found the magistrates ready to make most of the concessions his Majesty had instructed

FACSIMILE OF THE KING'S PROCLAMATION FOR THE ARREST OF WHALLEY AND GOFFE

them to demand. But in Massachusetts they were utterly defeated of their purpose.

Colonel Nicolls could be very little with them, because he was engrossed in the pressing and necessary business of settling the government of the Duke's province of New York; and yet they were not permitted by their commission to take any official action without him. Sir Robert Carr and Colonel Cartwright were men wholly unfitted to transact business of delicacy and importance. They had neither tact nor weight of character, nor any knowledge or experience in such affairs as they now tried to handle; and they were dealing with astute men who knew every point of the controversy and every mooted question of law like parts of a familiar personal experience. The Massachusetts General Court had adopted a declaration of their rights by charter the very year they tardily proclaimed Charles II. king (1661), as if anticipating an attack upon their government. In it they had argued their right to a complete self-government, and had declared that they owed no further direct duty to the King than allegiance to his person, the safe-keeping of that part of his territories over which they exercised jurisdiction, the punishment of crime, and the protection of the Protestant religion; and they maintained nothing less now in the presence of the commissioners. It proved impossible to bring them to terms. The commissioners more than once put themselves in the wrong by a loss of temper or an unwarranted assumption of authority; and the whole matter had at last to be referred back, unsettled, to the King. A letter thereupon came out of England commanding Massachusetts to send agents over to deal with the authorities there; but they found a way to avoid obedience to the summons, and once again, as when their charter had been attacked thirty years before, the attention of statesmen at home was called off from their business to matters of more pressing consequence. Clarendon, who was the master spirit of the new policy of the government towards the colonies, too stout for prerogative to suit the Parliament, too stiff for right to suit the King, lost his place and was banished the kingdom in 1667, the year after the commissioners returned to England with their report of failure. The Dutch accepted the gage of war thrown down by England's seizure of New Netherland, and the struggle widened until it threatened to become a general European conflict. Without Clarendon, politics dwindled in England to petty intrigue. There was time to take breath again at the Bay. Massachusetts was, it turned out, to keep her jealously guarded charter for nearly twenty years yet.

Here the chief *authorities* and *sources* are those already referred to under Sections I. to V. of this chapter.

THE Restoration and the reassertion of royal authority had done much to check the growth of Massachusetts and her neighbor colonies of the Puritan group, but it had noticeably stimulated settlement to the southward, near where Virginia lay with her Cavalier leaders; and even in New England a natural growth went slowly on. Clarendon had been statesman enough to see that the colonies in America were no longer petty settlements, lying outside the general scheme of national policy. He saw that they were now permanent parts of a growing empire, and he had sought until his fall to bring them under a general plan of administration, which the commissioners of 1664 were to take the first step towards setting up. America was no longer merely a place of refuge for Puritans and royalists, each in their turn, no longer merely a region of adventure for those whose fortunes desperately needed mending. It was henceforth to be a place of established enterprise and of steadfast endeavor pushed forward from generation to generation; and the steady advance of English settlement, showing itself now almost like the movement of a race, already sufficiently revealed what the future was to bring forth.

The capture of New Netherland, though it brought war upon England, seemed to secure peace for America. There was no longer, when Colonel Nicolls was done, an alien power between New England and Virginia. The whole coast was at last indisputably English land, all the way from the little settlements struggling for existence far to the north in the bleak forests which lay beyond the Massachusetts grant to Spain's lonely forts in the far south by the warm bays of Florida. That was a royal principality which the Duke of York had received from the lavish Charles,—all the great triangle of rich lands which spread northward and westward between the Connecticut and the lower waters and great Bay of the Delaware, Long Island, Nantucket, Martha's Vineyard, and all their neighbor islands, great and small, included,—and Colonel Nicolls had established his authority, at any rate at the centre of it, where the Dutch had been, in a way that gave promise of making it abundantly secure. But the Duke was a Stuart, and no statesman; loved authority, but was not provident in the use of it; and parted with much of the gift before it was fairly in his hands. Colonel Nicolls and his fellow commissioners did not take possession of New Amsterdam until August, 1664, and it was then nearly two months since the Duke had given a large

SIGNATURE OF GEORGE CARTERET

part of New Netherland away to his friends Lord John Berkeley, Baron of Stratton, and Sir George Carteret, of Saltrum.

Late in June he had granted to these gentlemen,

his close associates in friendship and in affairs, his colleagues in the Board of Admiralty, over which he presided, all his own rights and powers within that part of his prospective territory which lay to the south of 41° 40′ north latitude and between the Delaware River and the sea, touching the Hudson and the harbor of New York at the north, and ending at Cape May in the south. This new province he called New Jersey, in compliment to Sir George Carteret, who had been governor of the island of Jersey when the Parliament was arrayed against the King, and who had held it long and gallantly for his royal master. Colonel Nicolls, the Duke's able governor in New York, knew nothing of the grant of New Jersey until the ship *Philip* actually put into the harbor in July, 1665, bringing a few settlers for the new province and Philip Carteret, a kinsman of Sir George's, to be its governor. Colonel Nicolls had but just completed his careful organization of the Duke's possessions; had put his best gifts of foresight and wise moderation into the settlement of their affairs, to the satisfaction of the numerous Dutch as well as of the less numerous English established there; and was not a little chagrined to see a good year's work so marred by his improvident master's gift. There was nothing for it, however, but to accept the situation and receive the representative of the new proprietors with as good a grace as possible, like a soldier and a gentleman. Knowing nothing of the grant to Berkeley and Carteret, he had already authorized a settlement at Elizabethtown, on the shore that lay nearest to Staten Island to the westward, and had granted rights and titles to other purchasers who had settled on the southern shore of the great outer Bay, near Sandy Hook; and the new colonists there now discontentedly doubted what their rights would be.

Much the larger part of the population of the original province of New Netherland, however, still remained under the authority of Colonel Nicolls and "the Duke's Laws," notwithstanding the setting apart of New Jersey to be another government,—in one direction, indeed, more than the Dutch themselves had pretended to govern; for the Duke's possessions included all of Long Island, the portion which lay beyond Oyster Bay and which had been conceded by the Dutch to the English in 1655, as well as the parts which lay close about the bay at New York. There were probably about seven thousand souls, all told, in New Netherland when the English took it, and of these fifteen hundred lived in the little village which was drawn close about the fort at New Amsterdam. The rest were near at hand on Long Island and on Staten Island, or were scattered up and down the lands which lay upon the Hudson on either hand as far as Fort Orange, which Colonel Nicolls renamed "Albany," because James was Duke of York and Albany. The Swedes, also, who had settled on the South River (the Delaware), and whom Stuyvesant had conquered, had built for the most part on the western bank of the river, and were outside the bounds of New Jersey. On the eastern bank, where Lord Berkeley and Sir George Carteret were to be proprietors, there were but a handful of Dutch and Swedes at most. These, with the little Dutch hamlets which stood near New York on the western bank of the Hudson, at Weehawken, Hoboken, Pavonia, Ahasimus, Constable's Hook, and Bergen, and the new homes of the English families whom Colonel Nicolls had authorized to settle within the grant at Elizabethtown and by the Hook, contained all the subjects the new proprietors could boast.

The government which the proprietors instructed Philip Carteret to establish was as liberal and as sensible as that which Colonel Nicolls had set up in New York. On the day on which they appointed their governor they

SIGNATURE OF PHILIP CARTERET

had signed a document which they called "The Concessions and Agreements of the Lords Proprietors of New Jersey, to and with all and every of the adventurers and all such as shall settle and plant there," and which offered not only gifts of land upon most excellent good terms to settlers, but religious toleration also and a free form of government. "The Duke's Laws," which Colonel Nicolls had set up for the government of New York, were equally liberal in matters of religion, but not in matters of self-government. The New Jersey lords proprietors directed their governor to associate with himself in the administration of the province a council of his own choosing not only, but also an assembly of twelve representatives, to be chosen annually by the freemen of the province. This assembly was to make the laws of the colony, and no tax was to be laid without its consent. The governor and his council were to appoint only freeholders of the colony to office, —unless the assembly assented to the appointment of others. It did not seem necessary to call an assembly at once; the scattered hamlets could separately attend to their own simple affairs well enough until more settlers should come. The first years of the new governor's rule were quietly devoted to growth.

The governor established himself and the thirty odd settlers and servants who came with him at the new hamlet just begun at Elizabethtown; and the next year, 1666, the *Philip* brought other settlers to join them. The governor took pains to make known the liberal terms of settlement he was authorized to offer, in New England and elsewhere in the colonies already established, as well as at home in England. A steady drift of colonists, accordingly, began to set his way. In 1666 the Elizabethtown tract was divided to make room for other settlements at Woodbridge and Piscataway. The same year numerous families from Milford, Guilford, Branford, and New Haven came and began to make homes for themselves at Newark, on the Passaic, —dissatisfied with the condition of affairs on the Sound since they had been tied to the Hartford government, and determined to have a free home of their own where only church members of their own way of thinking and of worship should have the right to vote or to hold office. It was a very notable migration, made in organized companies, as the first settlements upon the Sound had been, and sapped the New Haven towns of their old stock. "The men, the methods, the laws, the officers, that made New Haven town what it was in 1640, disappeared from the Connecticut colony, but came to full life again immediately in New Jersey." Even Mr.

243

Davenport left the familiar seat he had himself chosen and returned in his old age to Boston. By April, 1668, New Jersey seemed to the governor ready for its first assembly, and he called upon the freemen to make their choice of representatives.

The Puritans of the new settlements controlled the assembly when it came together at Elizabethtown the next month (26 May, 1668) and passed a bill of pains and penalties against various sorts of offenders which was drawn in some of its parts directly from the Book of Leviticus, as an earnest of their intentions in matters of government; but they had been in session scarcely four days when they grew impatient to be at home again, and adjourned. When they met a second time, in November, the little hamlets on the Delaware, which had not sent delegates to the first session, were represented; but the people of the "Monmouth grant," by Sandy Hook, were not. They were angry because Governor Carteret had refused to acknowledge their right to make rules of local government for themselves, under the terms of their grant from Colonel Nicolls, given before the New Jersey grant was known of in New York; and they declared that the persons who had assumed to act for them at the first session of the assembly, in May, had had no real authority to do so. The representatives who did attend the November sitting soon went home again, dissatisfied that the governor's council did not associate itself with them closely enough in the conduct of the assembly's business, and impeded, as they thought, the execution of the provisions of the "Concessions," the great document which was their constitution from the proprietors. It was to be many years yet, as it turned out, before the conduct of the government of the colony

LOADING SHIPS IN ALBEMARLE SOUND

was to be satisfactorily provided for. The several scattered settlements had little sympathy with each other, and New Jersey was not yet a complete or organized colony.

It was a day of new proprietary grants to gentlemen in favor at court; but the making of grants was very different from the making of governments. At the very time when Governor Carteret was trying to form a government that would hold the scattered towns of New Jersey together in some sort of discipline and order, the representatives of another proprietary government of the same kind were trying the same experiment with much the same fortune in the south on the "Carolina" grant, which the King had made the year before he gave New Netherland to his brother. In 1663 he had granted the lands which lay south of Virginia between the thirty-first and the thirty-sixth degrees of north latitude to eight proprietors: the great Earl of Clarendon, General George Monk, now Duke of Albemarle, William Lord Craven, Anthony Lord Ashley (soon to be Earl of Shaftesbury), Sir John Colleton, John Lord Berkeley and Sir George Carteret, to whom the Duke of York was the next year to give New Jersey, and Sir William Berkeley, brother of Lord John and governor of Virginia. Here, as in New Jersey, settlers had long ago entered and begun a life of their own. The Virginians had spoken of the region hitherto as "South Virginia," and it was some of their own people who had begun its settlement. In 1653 Roger Greene had taken a hundred settlers to the coast of the broad Sound which was afterwards to be called Albemarle,—after the great General Monk's new ducal title,—and had established them on a grant at "Chowan," given to him by the Virginia House of

Burgesses as a reward for the "hazard and trouble of first discovery," and as an "encouragement of others for seating those southern parts of Virginia." Nine years later (1662) George Durant followed with other settlers, Quakers driven out of Maryland and Virginia, whom the Virginian authorities were glad to be rid of and have settled out of sight in the wilderness. They began to build to the eastward of Mr. Greene's people at "Chowan," upon the next peninsula of the same indented coast, in what was called the "Perquimans"

SIGNATURES OF CAROLINA PROPRIETORS

region. And then, the next year, 1663, the King handed their lands over to be governed by the eight lords proprietors of "Carolina."

There were by that time quite three hundred families settled there; and there were none besides in all the vast tract that the King's charter called "Carolina." These first comers had chosen for their settlements a region neither fertile nor wholesome. Great pine barrens stood there upon the coast, interspersed with broad swamps dense with a tangle of cypress and juniper. Inside the coast districts, where the land rose to drier levels and the virgin soils lay rich and wholesome, were some of the finest regions of all the continent, fertile and sweet-aired and full of inviting seats; but there was no highway to these. Only the sea and the rivers were open. The land was everywhere covered with untouched forests, pathless and unexplored. For the present settlers were obliged to content themselves with the flat, unwholesome coast, in spite of its killing fevers, because it alone was accessible. This Albemarle country was Virginia's frontier, the refuge of the restless, the unfortunate, and the discontented, and of all who found her laws and her power to enforce them irksome and unbearable. Some very steady and substantial people there were also, no doubt, who chose to live there,—like the good Quakers whom Mr. Durant had brought thither because they could find a welcome nowhere else. There was a good profit to be made out of timber cut from those splendid forests, and out of the breeding of cattle, which was easy enough; and many industrious families liked the steady trade of the region, with its accompaniment of a free life in the ungoverned wilderness. But it was as yet the shiftless, the irresponsible, and the adventurous who were most attracted.

What with adventurers who were ungovernable and men of industry and ability who wished to be let alone, it was not an easy or a promising place in which to set up the authority of proprietors who were in England and had done nothing to help the men whom they meant to govern. Sir William Berkeley, nevertheless, being himself one of the proprietors, took the first step towards making good the rights of the new masters in 1664, when, by the authority of his associates, he commissioned William Drummond to act as governor among the people at Chowan and Perquimans. The appointment of a governor made little difference at first. Not until three years later did the proprietors attempt the establishment of a regular government, and even then the arrangements which they made were very liberal. They

SEAL OF THE LORDS PROPRIETORS OF CAROLINA

that year, 1667, sent over Samuel Stephens from England to be governor in Drummond's place, and they sent with him a document of "Concessions," very like that which Lord Berkeley and Sir George Carteret, two of their number, had lately granted to the settlers in New Jersey. There was to be perfect freedom in religion; the elected representatives of the people were to make the laws of the settlements; no taxes were to be imposed without their consent; and they could assemble upon their own motion, without waiting for a summons from the governor. The governor was to have twelve councillors and the people were to have twelve representatives, as in New Jersey; but half of the governor's council were to be chosen by the assembly itself, and governor, councillors, and representatives were to sit together as a single body,—so that the people's delegates were sure of a majority in all its deliberations.

The assembly used its power to exempt all new-comers from taxes for a year after their coming, and to provide that for five years to come no suits should be heard for debts or any other obligations contracted outside Carolina. Of course such laws brought insolvent Virginian debtors and all sorts of Virginian outlaws in larger numbers than ever to the settlements, and the Virginians called the place "Rogues' Harbor"; but others of a better sort came also, and it was population first of all that the Albemarle law-makers wanted. A more settled life and a less irregular and questionable way of encouraging immigrants came afterwards in due time, —as well as unexpected troubles with the proprietors. The first grant. of 1663, had not in fact included the Albemarle settlements, though those who framed it supposed that it did; but in 1665 a new charter was obtained which advanced the boundary line far enough northward to make sure of including them. And then the proprietors, having a taste for a more elaborate way of governing, adopted a highly complicated and detailed plan, drawn up by Mr. John Locke, who was then, at thirty-seven, secretary to Anthony Lord Ashley, one of the proprietors. The document contained eighty-one articles, was called the "Fundamental Constitutions" of Carolina, and was elaborate enough for a populous kingdom. It bore date 21 July, 1669.

The proprietors were too much men of the world and of affairs to suppose that that simple community, only just now begun, was ready for an elaborate government, which, among other things, proposed to change

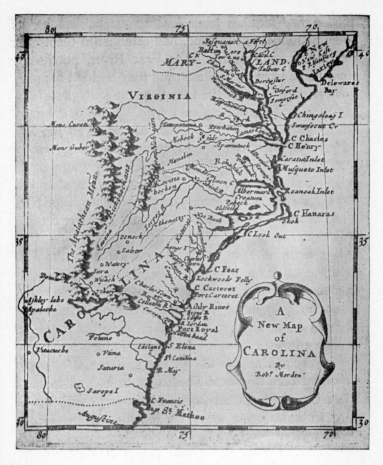

MAP OF CAROLINA, 1687

very radically the free tenure of the land into a sort of
feudal holding under hereditary nobles; but they meant
to establish their system when they could, and were in
too great haste, it turned out, to believe that parts of
it could at once be made to apply.   Even yet "Carolina"
had no settlements except those at Albemarle.   In

251

1660 a few families from Massachusetts, looking for some betterment of fortune, had established themselves near the mouth of the Cape Fear River, purchasing their lands from the Indians; but they had left the place disheartened in 1663, the very year the lords proprietors got their first grant from the crown. News of the grant stimulated some of the English who were in the Barbadoes to attempt the same thing that the Massachusetts men had attempted. In May, 1664, they began a settlement upon a new site, far up the spreading stream of the Cape Fear. But three years were enough for them also; in 1667 they, too, were gone, and the river country was again empty.

It proved no light matter to govern even the little settlements at Albemarle. The publication there of the formidable Fundamental Constitutions in 1673, when the proprietors seemed bent upon putting them at any rate partially into operation, disturbed the as yet unfettered settlers very deeply,—for they loved and meant to have a free life in the wilderness. Though they had been promised freedom of belief and worship, these Constitutions, as published among them, threatened to make every man pay for the maintenance of the Church of England as an established church. Moreover, the air was at that very time full of disquieting rumors. News came that the King had given all of Virginia to Lords Arlington and Culpeper,—not to rule, indeed, but to own; and it was said that the proprietors of Carolina meant to divide the province among themselves, and give the Albemarle country to Sir William Berkeley, whom they would have exceedingly disrelished as their master, being quit, as they had hoped, of Virginia's imperious governor. Worst of all, the governor whom the proprietors had sent them sided with the King's officers in enforcing the Navigation Acts, whose enforcement would spoil their trade. They sold their timber and their cattle very freely to shrewd skippers out of New England, who brought them what they needed from the ports of the Puritan colonies, got their timber and cattle, disposed of them in the West Indies, and came back again thence with good cargoes of sugar, rum, and molasses, for which they took tobacco, to be sold at home for export into England,—all without license from the crown and in plain defiance of the Acts.

The colonists preferred their trade to the laws of Parliament, and their freedom to the laws of the lords proprietors. Moreover, the very charter under which the proprietors acted had given their lordships the right to make laws and constitutions only "by and with the advice, consent, and approbation of the freemen" of the colony, or their representatives; and these new regulations had never been so approved or ratified. The temper of resistance among the colonists proved more than the agents of the lords proprietors could manage; and for almost ten years after the publication of the "Constitutions" the settlers at Albemarle took leave to have their own way upon every critical occasion. In 1675 their governor, Carteret, Stephens's successor, went to England in a sort of despair, to explain that he was not allowed to govern. In 1677 the colonists seized the collector of the revenues, and several thousand pounds of the revenue with him, because he tried to break up their trade with New England and the West Indies. They were quieter without a governor than with one, and meant to obey authority only on their own terms.

The proprietors were to find that it was not much easier to govern settlements of their own planting than to govern the rough-and-ready hamlets at Albemarle, which had been set up without them. By August, 1669, the month after they signed the first draft of their Fundamental Constitutions, they had an expedition ready to go into the southern parts of Carolina and plant a colony which should be worth helping and worth governing; and by April of the next year it was actually planted. There had been many disasters to face by the way. The settlers had been kept a long time at the Barbadoes, to repair their ships and get supplies, and colonists to recruit their number; and they had come away from the islands with Colonel William Sayle, a man stricken in years, for governor, instead of Sir John Yeamans, who knew the coast and was in the full vigor of manhood. The aged soldier who took them to their place of settlement had founded a colony of Presbyterians in the Barbadoes twenty years ago, and still showed not a little of the steadfastness and strength of purpose that had marked him for a leader then; but he was too old for this new task, and died the next year in the doing of it. The place chosen for the settlement was a pleasing bluff within the fair Kiawah River,—which they presently called the Ashley, in honor of the distinguished nobleman for whom Mr. Locke had written the Fundamental Constitutions. Their settlement they called Charlestown; and there they lived for ten years without notable incident, except that Sir John Yeamans, who was their governor from 1671–1674, brought negro slaves with him when he came from the Barbadoes in 1672. Mr. Joseph West was governor most of the time during the first years of settlement, and ruled very sensibly, assisted by a council of which the freemen of the colony elected a part. Things went quietly enough

EARL OF SHAFTESBURY

until the proprietors and the government at home bestirred themselves to enforce the Fundamental Constitutions and the laws of trade.

255

It was no mere perverseness of temper or mere love of license that set the colonists so stubbornly against the plans and the authority of their governors. It was rather their practical sense and their knowledge of their own necessities. They knew that, if they were to thrive at all, they must be let live as they could in the wilderness, as the actual and inevitable conditions of their own lives permitted, not cramped by elaborate constitutions or by the rigid restrictions imposed by the Parliament's laws of trade, but with a freedom suitable to their rough and simple ways of living. Virginia herself, for all she was so much older, so staid and loyal, was moved to revolt almost as easily as Albemarle and Charlestown when put upon more grossly than she could bear. She was herself in rebellion at the very time the men at Albemarle were openly defying their governor to put into force among them the laws which forbade their trade with the Indies.

Virginians had seen their burdens and their grievances against the government alike of their governor and of the King grow ominously heavier and heavier ever since the Restoration, which they had once deemed so happy an event, until at last the condition in which they found themselves seemed quite intolerable. Sir William Berkeley was no longer the manly, approachable gentleman he had been in the earlier time of his first governorship,—bluff and wilful, but neither bitter nor brutal. The long days of his enforced retirement, while the Commonwealth stood (1652–1660), had soured his temper and alienated him from the life of the colony; and he had come out of it to take up the government again, not a Virginian, like the chief Cavalier gentlemen about him, who now accounted Virginia their home and neighborhood, but a harsh and arbitrary servant of the crown and of his own interests, ready to fall into a rage at the slightest contradiction, suave only when he meant to strike.

The change was not obvious at first; but it became evident enough ere long. The King recommended mere

ST. PETER'S CHURCH, KENT COUNTY, VIRGINIA

place hunters and adventurers to Sir William for appointment in Virginia, wishing to be rid of them, or to pay his personal obligations at Virginia's cost. Sir William put them in office in the colony, and along with them his own friends, kinsmen, and favorites, until councillors, sheriffs, magistrates, surveyors, customs clerks, the whole civil service of Virginia, seemed a body of covetous placemen who meant to thrive whether

justice were done and the laws kept or not. Nor was
that the worst of it. It was next to impossible for the
small planter, or for any man who did not thrive exceedingly, to pay the growing taxes and the innumerable petty exactions which were demanded of him to pay
these men, satisfy the King's collectors, and maintain
the expensive government of the colony. The Navigation Acts forbade the colonists to send their tobacco
anywhere but to England, in English ships, and so
the English skippers could demand what freight they
pleased and the English merchants could buy the tobacco
at such prices as suited them. The same Acts forbade
any goods to be brought into the colonies except from
England, and so the English merchants could exact
what they chose for the supplies they sent and the skippers could get their return freight charges. There was
no coin in Virginia, or next to none; tobacco itself, her
principal crop, served as money, and when it was worth
little and the goods it was used to pay for were worth a
great deal, it was hard to live at all, and poverty seemed
a thing enacted and enforced.

Time had been, before the meddlesome Acts of Navigation, when the Dutch ships which came in at the river paid
five shillings on every anchor of brandy they brought
in, and ten shillings on every hogshead of tobacco they
took out; and the money had been appropriated to make
good the defence of the frontier against the Indians.
But no Dutch skippers came in since the Acts, and that
charge also fell upon the poor planters. "It hath so
impoverished them," declared Mr. Bland, of London
(1677), looking for the sake of untrammelled trade into
these matters, "that they scarce can recover wherewith
to cover their nakedness." Taxes were not levied upon

A

BRIEF HISTORY
OF THE
VVARR

With the *INDIANS* in
NEVV-ENGLAND,

(From *June* 24, 1675. when the firſt Engliſh-man was murdered by the Indians, to *Auguſt* 12. 1676. when *Philip,* aliàs
Metacomet, the principal Author and Beginner
of the Warr, was ſlain.)
Wherein the Grounds, Beginning, and Progreſs of the Warr,
is ſummarily expreſſed.

TOGETHER WITH A SERIOUS
EXHORTATION

to the Inhabitants of that Land,

By *INCREASE MATHER,* Teacher of a Church of
Chriſt, in *Boſton* in *New-England.*

Levit. 26 25. *I will bring a Sword upon you, that ſhall avenge the quarrel of the Co-
venant.*
Pſal. 107 43. *Whoſo is wiſe and will obſerve thoſe things, even they ſhall underſtand the
Loving-kindneſs of the Lord.*
Jer. 22. 15. *Did not thy Father doe Judgment and Juſtice, and it was well with him?*

Segnius irritant animos demiſſa per aures,
Quàm quæ ſunt oculis commiſſa ſidelibus.   *Horat.*
Lege Hiſtoriam ne fias Hiſtoria.   *Cic.*

BOSTON,   Printed and Sold by *John Foſter* over
againſt the Sign of the *Dove.* 1 6 7 6.

TITLE-PAGE OF INCREASE MATHER'S "BRIEF HISTORY OF THE WARR
WITH THE INDIANS"

THE

Widdow Ranter

OR,

The HISTORY of

Bacon in Virginia.

A

TRAGI-COMEDY

Acted by their Majesties Servants.

Written by Mrs. A. Behn.

LONDON, Printed for James Knapton at the
Crown in St. Paul's Church-Yard. 1690.

TITLE-PAGE OF MRS. APHRA BEHN'S "WIDDOW RANTER"

the land, so that each man might pay in proportion to his property, but by the poll, each man alike, and every servant assessed with his master; so that the poor man bore the chief burden, and sweated under it intolerably. His tobacco, with the diminishing price the English merchants put upon it, was all he had to pay with, and seemed every leaf of it to go to the tax gatherer,—who got his office by favor, and himself took ten *per cent.* of what he collected. Members of the governor's council were exempt from the poll tax, with ten servants apiece, and yet were paid salaries out of the taxes. The government seemed a thing planned for the support and behoof of "the grandees" of the governor's court, the men of the Virginian democracy said, and their discontent grew with their numbers. Their numbers grew fast enough. There were six thousand white indentured servants in the colony. Every year quite fifteen hundred of these saw the hoped-for end of their term of service come, and were given fifty acres of land apiece to shift for themselves and join the ranks of taxpayers. When the price of tobacco fell, one evil year, to a halfpenny a pound, Mr. Ludwell declared to the governor that nothing but "faith in the mercy of God, loyalty to the King, and affection for the government" restrained them from rebellion. And their affection for the government cooled fast enough.

The restrictions put upon the carrying trade had but the other day been made complete in their kind. In 1672 an act for the still "better securing of the plantation trade" had forbidden even a coastwise trade among the colonies themselves, or with the English Bermudas, in sugar, tobacco, cotton, wool, indigo, or any other of the enumerated articles of the former Acts, except they were first taken into England, or paid at the port of export the duties levied at the English wharves.

As if poverty, and heavy taxes to make it the more burdensome, were not enough, deep anxiety lest Virginia should lose even the forms of her liberty was added, and finally war with the Indians, to make the measure full to overflowing. It was useless to appeal to the House of Burgesses for a redress of grievances, because Sir William Berkeley would allow no election of a new House. For fifteen years he kept alive the House which had been chosen in 1661, at the time of the Restoration. It was made up of hearty partisans of the King's government, as was natural, having been chosen when it was, and was quite ready to follow Sir William's lead in most things. He would adjourn its sessions from time to time, but would not dissolve it; and so there were no elections at all. The Burgesses themselves were content enough to prolong its life, and keep the governor in good humor by their votes. Each member received two hundred and fifty pounds of tobacco for every day he spent in the assembly, to keep himself, his servant, and a horse; every committee of the assembly had its paid clerk and money out of the colonial treasury for its liquors; and there was oftentimes more profit to be got out of a long session than out of diligent tobacco planting at home.

In 1673 came the news that the King had given all Virginia to Lords Arlington and Culpeper, to be their proprietary province, like Carolina and New Jersey, and several gentlemen had to be sent over to England in haste to plead, intrigue, and protest, as if for the very life of the colony, against such a usurpation. Their lordships kept the royal quit-rents, spite of all opposition, and a new poll tax of sixty pounds of tobacco a head had to be levied to pay the expenses of the com-

LORD CULPEPER

missioners sent to plead the colony's case against them. And then, in 1675, when affairs seemed most darkened and confused by selfish and arbitrary action both at home and over sea, there came hot trouble with the Indians, which the governor refused either to deal with himself or allow others to settle.

It was that that brought the explosion. A sort of desperate wrath took possession of the stronger and more daring spirits of the colony, and they presently found a leader who gave Sir William good cause to fear what might come of their anger. The governor ought to have remembered that other year of blood, 1644, when last the Indians were on the war-path, and how sad a blow it had dealt the colony. True, there had then been scarcely ten thousand people in Virginia, and there were now no doubt close upon fifty thousand, armed and able in all ordinary straits to take care of themselves. It was not likely the Indians could strike very far within the borders or threaten the heart of the colony. But men and women and children lived on the borders no less than at the heart of the colony. Precious lives could be wasted there as well as elsewhere, —plain people, no doubt, but Englishmen,—and the colonists were not likely to stand tamely by and look on at the massacre of their own people. No doubt the Indians had been unwisely, unjustly dealt with and provoked, goaded to hostile acts by attacks upon one tribe for what, it may be, another had done; such things had too often happened, and the colonists were not over-careful to avoid them. But that was no reason for refusing to put a force into the field to stop the massacres. What was the governor's scruple? He alone could grant licenses to trade with the Indians, and he did not grant them for nothing. It was something more than a surmise that he shared the profits of the trade, and let the traders sell what they would to the savages,

ON THE WAR-PATH

though it were firearms and powder and shot, against the laws of the colony, to make the profits worth while. Did he hesitate to interrupt his lucrative fur trade with the redmen; or was he reluctant to put any armed force into the field for fear of what it might do for the redress of grievances within the colony after the danger from the Indians had been made an end of? Whatever his motive, he would not act, and could not, he said, until the assembly came together for its regular meeting in March, 1676. Meanwhile scores of people had been murdered, plantation after plantation had been destroyed (sixty in a single county within a space of little more than two weeks), and the border was desolate and terror-stricken. And even when March came and the meeting of the Burgesses, Berkeley played them false. The assembly met, the "Long Assembly" elected fifteen years ago,—met for the last time, as it turned out,—and voted to send a force of five hundred men against the savages; but Berkeley disbanded the little army before it could take the field; and defence was again abandoned.

Here was more than could be endured; and there were men in Virginia who were ready to defy the governor and get their rights by arms. Nathaniel Bacon had sworn with a hot oath that if the redskins meddled with him he would harry them, commission or no commission; and he kept his threat. He was of the hot blood that dares a great independence. He was great-grandson of Sir Thomas Bacon, of Friston Hall, Suffolk, cousin to the great Lord Bacon, of whose fame the world had been full these fifty years; and though he was but nine-and-twenty, study at the Inns of Court and much travel in foreign lands had added to his gentle breeding the popular manners and the easy self-confidence of a man of the world before he turned his back upon England and came with his young wife to be a planter on James River in Virginia. In May news came that the Indians had attacked his own upper plantation and had murdered his overseer and one of his favorite servants; and he did not hesitate what to do. A company of armed and mounted men begged him to go with them against the redskins, and he led them forth upon their bloody errand without law or license, member of the governor's council and magistrate though he was. He sent to ask the governor for a commission, indeed, but he did not turn back, or lose his armed following either, when word was brought that the governor had refused it, and had proclaimed him and all with him to be outlaws. It was flat rebellion; but Bacon's pulse only quickened at that, and Virginia for a little while seemed his to command.

He put a stirring tragedy upon the stage there in the quiet colony with its sombre forests, and played it out with a dash and daring that must take every generous man's imagination who remembers how fair and winning a figure the young leader made through all those uneasy days, and how irresistibly he caught the eye and the fancy with the proud way in which he carried himself, lithe and tall and dark of skin, and that melancholy light in his dusky eyes, a man of action and of passion,—such passion as it moves and wins other men to look upon. That was a summer to be remembered in which he pushed to the front in affairs,—and most of all its sad ending.

Berkeley found that he could not openly treat Bacon as a rebel without kindling a flame of discontent on

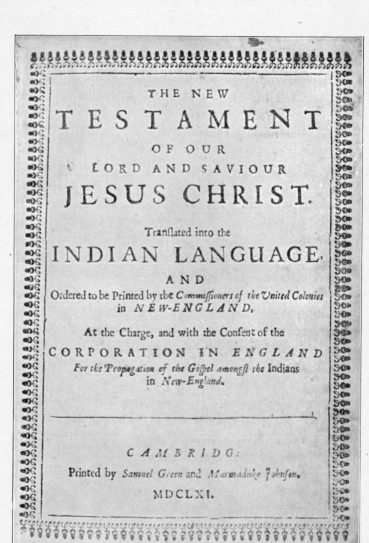

THE NEW TESTAMENT

OF OUR

LORD AND SAVIOUR

JESUS CHRIST.

Translated into the

INDIAN LANGUAGE,

AND

Ordered to be Printed by the *Commissioners of the United Colonies* in *NEW-ENGLAND,*

At the Charge, and with the Consent of the

CORPORATION IN ENGLAND

For the Propagation of the Gospel amongst the Indians in *New-England.*

CAMBRIDG:

Printed by *Samuel Green* and *Marmaduke Johnson.*

MDCLXI.

TITLE-PAGE OF ELIOT'S ALGONQUIN VERSION OF THE NEW TESTAMENT every hand among the colonists. He was obliged to dissolve the "Long Assembly," call a new one, admit Bacon himself to a seat in it, hear his bad administration debated, and consent at last to the levying of an effective force to fight the Indians. But what he could not do openly he tried to do secretly and by treachery. One night while the assembly still sat Nathaniel Bacon fled from Jamestown, warned that his life was in danger. He returned with six hundred men at his back and compelled the governor to give him a commission. Once more he was proclaimed an outlaw, and all his followers outlaws with him, the moment he had turned his back and plunged into the Indian country; and a war for protection turned to civil war.

Bacon's blows were quick and terrible, and more to be feared than his biting speech. He had wellnigh exterminated the Indian tribe of Susquehannocks before he heard of or heeded his outlawry. Then he turned in his hot anger against the government itself, as if it had declared war upon him. He required and took of his followers an oath to resist not only the governor, but the very troops of the King himself should they come, until wrongs should be righted; and Berkeley was driven, a fugitive, to the far counties beyond the Bay. When he returned with a motley force to Jamestown he was driven forth again, and Jamestown was burned. Only Bacon's death ended the ugly business. As autumn approached he sickened and died (the first day of October, 1676), overcome by the passion of action and of feeling, and the exhausting life of the camp and the field; and his followers dispersed.

He had gone too far. At first, rank and file, no doubt, had been with him, men of substance with the rest, for

NATHANIEL BACON AND HIS FOLLOWERS BURNING JAMESTOWN

the right to live and to better the government; but most of the chief planters had held aloof even then; and as he went on they were more and more alienated. It became more and more an affair of the rabble, of the men who were poor and desperate and had nothing to lose. When he burned Jamestown he also sacked the plantations of the greater land-owners thereabouts, knowing them to be his enemies; and he died with the spirit of the outlaw too much kindled within him by the lawless work he had done, almost determined to withstand the King as well as the governor, and to make those who had not joined him pay for his work of resistance and reform,—no longer merely a champion of reasonable reformation, but a revolutionist. Nothing less could have alienated his friends, broken his party, and given Berkeley his full time of revenge against those whose cause had been just.

That revenge was only too complete. A fleet arrived out of England in January, 1677, with a regiment of the King's troops aboard, and commissioners to settle the troubles in the colony to the re-establishing of order; and the commissioners had themselves to rebuke and restrain the insensate bitterness of the maddened governor. He had set the hangman to work before they came, and by the time January was out had sent more than twenty persons to the gallows for their participation in the rebellion; among the rest William Drummond, the capable Scotsman whom he had deputed to be the first governor of the settlements at Albemarle, and who had governed very quietly there, knowing the men he had to deal with, but who was now in Virginia again, Mr. Bacon's friend and counsellor. "As I live," cried the King, when he learned the news from Virginia, "the old fool has put to death more people in that naked country than I did for the murder of my father"; and he showed little patience when the old man came home to make his peace. The King would not see him, and the broken governor was dead,—of chagrin, men said,—by midsummer (1677). Virginia was rid of him; forgot how well she had liked him at first; and remembered without compunction how her people had celebrated his departure with bonfires and the booming of cannon.

It was in that year, 1677, when Virginia's rebellion was over and her chief rebels hanged, that the heady settlers at Albemarle rose against the proprietors and the Acts of trade, thrust their governor out, and seized three thousand pounds of the customs revenue. They were but four thousand people, all told, but they were all of one mind, and did what Mr. Bacon could not do. For two years they governed themselves, upon such a model as might have pleased Virginia's rebel. William Drummond, who had lived among them, had led Mr. Bacon to hope, and half expect, that these Albemarle men would send him aid and make common cause with him against the power of a royal governor and rich land-owners; but they had saved their strength for themselves. They took little thought for Virginia; and they could not have helped Mr. Bacon to succeed had they wished to help him. He had rebelled against powers which were already firmly established and which were to dominate Virginia throughout all the rest of her youth and of her growth to maturity.

That notable immigration of royalist gentlemen that had been pouring into the colony these five-and-twenty years, and which had brought Mr. Bacon himself to

STRANGE NEWS

FROM

VIRGINIA:

Being a full and true

ACCOUNT

OF THE

LIFE and DEATH

OF

Nathanael Bacon Esquire,

Who was the only Cause and Original of all the late
Troubles in that COUNTRY.

With a full Relation of all the Accidents which have
happened in the late War there between the
Christians and Indians.

LONDON,

Printed for *William Harris*, next door to the Turn-
Stile without *Moor-gate*. 1677.

TITLE-PAGE OF "STRANGE NEWS FROM VIRGINIA"

Virginia, had inevitably transformed the character of the little commonwealth. Large estates multiplied faster than small ones. Estates descended from father to son by the rule of primogeniture and were kept together by the strict law of entail. The ruling part in affairs fell more and more, and as if by a sort of social law of nature, to men who believed in aristocratic privilege in matters of government and dreaded a democratic levelling. Being for the most part men of breeding and of honor, they were ready to condemn quite as heartily as Mr. Bacon himself the corrupt and headstrong ways into which Sir William Berkeley had fallen; but they deemed revolution rather a new disease than a good remedy, and left Mr. Bacon to find his recruits among those who had less at stake.

Virginia's government was singularly like the government to which these ruling gentlemen had been accustomed at home in England; and her most influential men were as certain to make up her governing class as were the country gentlemen of England to procure magistracies in their counties. The Long Assembly had made changes in the law which rendered their supremacy more certain than ever before. The rule in respect of every office was appointment, not election. Only the Burgesses were elected out of all who took part in the government of the colony, and it was fixed custom from of old to select them from the members of the county bench, whom the governor appointed. Even they were to be chosen henceforth, the Long Assembly had decreed, by the freeholders only, and not by the common vote of all free residents, as before the Restoration. Local government was altogether in the hands of the ruling class. The vestry was the governing and direct-

GOVERNOR BERKELEY CONDEMNING WILLIAM DRUMMOND TO DEATH

ing body in every parish, and its twelve members were
to be chosen now in each parish, since the Long Assembly's law of 1662, not by free election, as in the old days,
but by the vote of the vestry itself, which was henceforth to fill its own vacancies. The county courts were
made up of magistrates appointed by the governor;
the sheriffs were nominated by the county courts, who
always named some one of their own number; for a long
time it had been the custom to elect one or more of the
county magistrates to represent the county in the House
of Burgesses; the county militia was organized under
lieutenants,—one for each county,—who were commonly chosen from among the members of the governor's
council. There was no place for any but men of means
and influence in such a government.

It was not an exclusive aristocracy. The life of the
colony was too simple, too essentially democratic for
that. Magistrates and vestrymen, sheriffs and county
lieutenants, all felt themselves neighbors and fellows
of the men they governed and took taxes of in those
quiet river neighborhoods. They were really representatives of the people they ruled, in temper and interest, if not in estate. They knew how their neighbors
lived,—as Mr. Jefferson explained long afterwards, in
behalf of the like magistrates of his own day,—because
they did not live very differently themselves. Their
motive to do their duty justly and well was the sufficient
motive of pride and self-respect, their desire for the
esteem of the people about them in the intimate life of
the rural country-side. Their rule was mild and public-spirited for the most part, more and more so as the life
of the colony settled to a fixed and stable order, and the
men who found their way into the vestry and the county

magistracy were generally men whom all esteemed and looked up to. But their rule was the rule of men of property, in favor of maintaining authority, sure to discountenance irregular attempts at radical reform; and Mr. Bacon's rebellion was the last of its kind. It had come too late, and was never repeated.

It was not this government of the "country gentlemen," at any rate, that had brought on the fatal troubles with the redskins which had stirred Mr. Bacon to his first act of rebellion; for New England also, self-governed and free as yet, had had her own struggle with the Indians, even more terrible and bitter, which had ended that same eventful summer of 1676. The New England Indians had not forgotten the fate of the Pequots; but that was now close upon forty years ago; the terror of it was no longer fresh, and their own situation had meantime grown a bit desperate. They were being shut within intolerably narrow bounds, and they could not move away from the regions where the English were slowly crowding them from their hunting-grounds without invading the territory of other tribes who would have no welcome for them. The white men paid for the lands they took, but they did not permit the redmen to refuse to sell. They played the part of masters always, and there could be no hope of better times to come. Devoted missionaries had come among the tribes from the white settlements and had won many of them to believe in the gospel of the true God; but their preaching was like the telling of idle fables to most of the reticent, intractable people of the forest, and left them untouched. They were ready at last when a leader should arise to plot for an uprising and a last trial of strength with the invading palefaces. Such a

leader arose in the person of Philip, the chief of the
Wampanoags, whom the English had penned up with-
in the narrow peninsula of Good Hope by the Bay of
Narragansett. The flame which Philip kindled among

KING PHILIP'S MARK

the Wampanoags promptly spread to the Narragansetts
and the Nipmucks, until it burned on every border, and
New England saw a day of terror such as she had
never seen before. There was no trouble like Virginia's. No governor hesitated, no armed force lacked
authority to do its work of protection and attack, no
levy lagged or was tardy; the country rallied to the
awful business. The fatal uprising began in June,
1675, and was ended,—for those tribes at least,—by
August, 1676, as the Pequot war had ended, with the
annihilation of the offending tribes. Those that were
not killed or taken were driven forth in hopeless flight;
those that were taken were sold as slaves in the West
Indies. Thereafter there were only the tribes in the
north to reckon with. But the white men's loss was
almost as great as that of the savages. More than one-
half of the towns of Massachusetts and Plymouth had
seen the torch and the tomahawk that awful year;
twelve of them had been utterly destroyed; no fewer
than six hundred buildings, chiefly dwellings, had been
burned; six hundred men had lost their lives, and
scores of women and children; debts had been piled up

and damage suffered which it would take years of bitter toil to pay and repair; and New England was for a little like a place desolate and stricken. But she ral-

OLD HOUSE IN DOCK SQUARE, BOSTON

lied in time, as always before, and slowly worked her way to better days, like the old days for peace and prosperity. Her dangers and anxieties were, at any rate, lessened in one matter that had often seemed to hold fear and danger permanently at its heart.

280

The chief general *authorities* for the history of New Jersey in the seventeenth century are Mr. William A. Whitehead's *East Jersey under the Proprietary Government, Contributions to East Jersey History,* and *The English in East and West Jersey, 1664–1689,* in Winsor's *Narrative and Critical History of America,* volume III.; Mr. Berthold Fernow's *Middle Colonies* in the fifth volume of Winsor; the first and second volumes of Bancroft and the second volume of Hildreth ; the second volume of Bryant and Gay's *Popular History of the United States ;* Andrew D. Mellick's *Story of an Old Farm ;* Austin Scott's *New Jersey,* in the *American Commonwealth Series ;* and Francis B. Lee's *New Jersey as a Colony and as a State,* 4 volumes.

The chief *sources* are to be found in the archives of the State of New Jersey ; Leaming and Spicer's *Grants, Concessions, and Original Constitutions of the Province of New Jersey, 1664–1682;* the *Collections* of the New Jersey Historical Society; and Samuel Smith's *History of the Colony of Nova Caesaria, or New Jersey, to 1721.*

The principal general *authorities* for the history of the Carolinas in the seventeenth century are Mr. J. A. Doyle's *English Colonies in America,* volume I.; William J. Rivers's *Sketch of the History of South Carolina* and *The Carolinas,* in the fifth volume of Winsor's *Narrative and Critical History of America ;* the first and second volumes of Bancroft and the second volume of Hildreth ; the second volume of Bryant and Gay's *Popular History of the United States ;* the second volume of John Fiske's *Old Virginia and Her Neighbours ;* Dr. Francis L. Hawks's *History of North Carolina ;* David Ramsay's *History of South Carolina, from its First Settlement in 1670 to the year 1808;* François X. Martin's *History of North Carolina, from the Earliest Period ;* and the valuable monographs, chiefly on the history of North Carolina, to be found in the *Johns Hopkins University Studies in Historical and Political Science.*

The chief *sources* for this period of the Carolinas are to be found in the *Colonial Records of North Carolina ;* Sainsbury's *Calendar of* [English] *State Papers, Colonial, V.;* B. R. Carroll's *Historical Collections of South Carolina,* which contain, among much more material of the first importance, Alexander Hewatt's *Historical Account of the Rise and Progress of the Colonies of South Carolina and Georgia,* originally published in London in 1779, John Archdale's account of the development of the colony to his own day, the portion of George Chalmers's *Political Annals of the Present United Colonies* which relates to Carolina, and Locke's *Funda-*

mental Constitution for Carolina; the *Charleston Year Books,* into which many valuable records, otherwise scattered, are brought together; Peter Force's *Tracts and Other Papers Relating to the Colonies in North America;* and Ben Perley Poore's *The Federal and State Constitutions, Colonial Charters, and other Organic Laws of the United States.*

THE troubles of Massachusetts did not end with the death of King Philip and the extermination of the hostile tribes. That very year of blood and terror, 1676, on the contrary, saw an old danger renewed. Mr. Edward Randolph arrived out of England commissioned to command the authorities of the colony to send agents over sea to answer for their assumption of power over the settlements to the north, beyond the bounds set by their charter, and in despite of the rights of those who were the legal proprietors there. It was the beginning of a very serious matter. She was to be brought to book at last for her too great independence, and her acts as if of sovereignty over the settlements about her. Poor as she was, after her awful struggle with the redskins, she hastened to buy out the rights of those who claimed proprietorship in Maine and New Hampshire (1677) for twelve hundred and fifty pounds sterling; but that only angered the wilful King the more and hastened graver difficulties. She was charged with illegally coining money, with persistently violating the Navigation Acts and trading as she pleased, with exercising whatever powers of government she desired without stopping first to find them granted to her in her charter; and there was little defence she could make in face of the plain facts. Again and again she sent capable agents to England to excuse her acts and justify them; but they made little impression upon the Privy Council or on the King's officers, and she was obliged in mere prudence to receive Mr. Randolph as the collector of customs, and speak submissively of the King's power.

At last there was an action of *quo warranto* against her (1683), and then a writ issued against her in the

NEW YORK CITY HALL AND DOCKS IN 1679

Court of Chancery, and in the end, October 23, 1684, an adverse judgment which declared her charter forfeited and her government returned to the crown. It was a bitter thing, but there was this time no escape from enduring it.

The same year, 1684, Virginia returned to her normal government again, as a royal province, and not the property of Lord Culpeper. The improvident King had not stopped with granting to Lords Arlington and

284

Culpeper, in 1672, "all the dominion of land and water called Virginia," and the quit-rents due from all the lands already occupied there; he had gone further, and in 1675 had appointed Lord Culpeper governor of the colony for life. Lord Culpeper had bought out the rights of Lord Arlington, his co-proprietor, and seemed commissioned at length to be Virginia's veritable sovereign master. But his career both as owner and as governor stopped very far short of the term of his life. By 1684 the King, tired of him, had withdrawn his commission and bought off his rights, leaving him a proprietary title over only the "Northern Neck" of Virginia, — the great peninsula which ran back to the mountains between the Potomac and the Rappahannock rivers; and the colony was again directly subject to the crown.

Lord Culpeper was little in his province even while his term as governor lasted. Sir Henry Chicheley was generally to be found acting in his stead,—a real Virginian, whom all esteemed a man of honor and of parts, a resident in the colony these twenty-five years, and for long either burgess or councillor, a neighbor and friend of the men he ruled as deputy to his lordship. Culpeper wished to be popular, and courted the goodwill of the colonists as he could; but a man without morals could not govern, and a man who would not stick at governing could not please the King, and his downfall was inevitable.

It was in the bad times of his rule that a new disorder fell upon the colony. In 1679 and 1680 the crops of tobacco were immense; there was more, much more, than could be sold, and its value fell so much that it was worth little or nothing to make purchases with,—

and yet it was the colony's chief currency. The assembly wished to stop or limit the planting of tobacco for a little, by statute; but the King, through the governor, forbade the restriction; and there suddenly broke forth a new sort of rebellion. In 1682 mobs of excited people swarmed upon plantation after plantation, destroying the growing crops of tobacco, until what would have filled ten thousand hogsheads had been cut up as it

NEW YORK ABOUT 1673

grew, and two hundred plantations had been laid waste within a single county. The armed forces of the colony stopped the riotous, lawless work at last; three of the ringleaders were tried and hanged, and order was restored; but it was made evident once again to what a temper things could be brought in Virginia when her people were not allowed to regulate their own affairs by orderly course of law; and the King's disgust with the rule of Lord Culpeper was not a little heightened.

Government by proprietors did not seem to go anywhere very well. Even Lord Baltimore found Maryland an uneasy property, and kept it only by consummate tact and watchful management. There were elements of every sort combined in its make-up. Not one-tenth

THE STRAND, NEW YORK, 1679

part of its people were of the proprietor's creed any longer; and not many besides Catholics were heartily and by choice of his party in affairs. At every change of political weather there was sure to be some sudden tempest or some covert insubordination there. In 1660 the assembly of the province, headed by Mr. Josias Fendall, the proprietor's own deputy, assumed sovereign

power till it should hear that the restoration of King
Charles was accomplished fact,—as the assembly in
Virginia did,—thinking the new King would be in no
mind to support a proprietor whom Cromwell also had
befriended. Only when it found the King Lord Baltimore's friend notwithstanding did it return to its allegiance. In 1675 Cecilius Lord Baltimore died, his
only son, Charles, succeeding; and the next year one
Davis and one Pate, taking their cue from Mr. Bacon
in Virginia, made bold themselves to head an actual
rebellion in arms. Their assembly, like Virginia's,
was chosen by freeholders only, contained a majority
whom the proprietor could command and would not part
with, and had ever since 1671, like Berkeley's favorite
Long Assembly, been kept alive by adjournment,—elections, apparently, having fallen out of favor on both
sides the border. The Indians were upon their frontier
also, and the taxes went, it seemed to the insurgents,
for nothing but to pay for offices provided for the en-
joyment of the proprietor's own kinsmen and adherents.
But success in Maryland depended upon success in
Virginia. When Mr. Bacon died, the Maryland insurgents yielded as promptly as the Virginian; Davis and
Pate went to the gallows; and there was an end of that.
But there was no ease in affairs even then. Maryland was not so readily to be kept in hand as Virginia.
Not her restless Puritans merely, but all her yeomen
also, of the rank and file, with their peculiar freedom
in local government, made her quick with the spirit as
if of a fretful and aggressive democracy. She had a
class of free tenants upon many of her estates who kept
alive throughout her country-sides a form of liberty
very ancient and very vital, and who made her life, so far

as they were concerned, very different indeed from that
of the country-sides of Virginia, where all alike looked
to the magistrates, the sheriffs, and the county lieutenants for government. Many a chief estate in Maryland
had its separate organization and its separate privilege
of self-government as a manor, under the terms of the
charter. In its court-leet, sitting under the presidency

A NEW YORK HOUSE IN 1679

of the steward, its freemen enacted their own local bye-
laws, chose their own constables and bailiffs, empanelled
their own juries, and put all petty offenders to their trial
and punishment. In its court-baron the freehold tenants
sat as judges of law and fact in matters of rent, tres-
pass, escheat, and the transfer of lands, not only in
suits among themselves, but in the settlement of their
rights as against their immediate lord the chief of the

manor as well. Here was a school of sturdy self-assertion transplanted out of the feudal law of old England into an air never breathed in the Middle Ages, and men of the lesser sort were heartened in their democracy accordingly. The barons of Baltimore had the self-confident tenants of many a miniature barony to deal with in their province; and had occasion to discover very often how vital a commonwealth it was that surged restless under their government.

Newer proprietors had not the advantage of their experience, and were always slow to see how uncommon a sort of property a colony was,—and that the high-spirited men who undertook to settle in colonies, like Englishmen everywhere, must be governed, if governed at all, under a free system which took note of their real circumstances and had their assent. Carolina furnished an example. There were, in fact, two Carolinas. Since the abandonment of the settlements which had for a little while struggled for a permanent foothold on the Cape Fear (1664–1667), there was nothing but unbroken wilderness through all the long reaches of silent forest which lay between the Albemarle country and the settlement at Charleston, — full two hundred and sixty miles as the crow flies. There could not well be one government for both these separated places, except in name; and it was difficult to tell which was the harder to govern. For almost a whole generation (1669–1698) the proprietors tried to force their Fundamental Constitutions upon them, but made no progress whatever in the matter. The list of proprietors was constantly changing. Some wearied of the business and sold their shares in it, some became bankrupt, some died. And governors changed more rapidly even than pro-

A Brief DESCRIPTION
OF
The Province
OF
CAROLINA
On the COASTS of FLOREDA.
AND
More perticularly of a *New-Plantation*
begun by the *ENGLISH* at *Cape-Feare,*
on that River now by them called *Charles-River,*
the 29ᵗʰ of *May,* 1664.

Wherein is set forth
The *Healthfulness* of the *Air*; the *Fertility* of
the *Earth*, and *Waters*; and the great *Pleasure* and
Profit will accrue to those that shall go thither to enjoy
the same.

Also,
Directions and advice to such as shall go thither whether
on their own accompts, or to serve under another.

Together with
A most accurate MAP of the whole *PROVINCE.*

London, Printed for *Robert Horne* in the first Court of *Gresham-
Colledge* neer *Bishopsgate street,* 1666.

TITLE-PAGE OF "A BRIEF DESCRIPTION OF THE PROVINCE OF
CAROLINA"

prietors,—no governor finding his seat very easy or being able to please both his masters in England and the colonists in Carolina. New proprietors brought no new wisdom, new governors no new capacity, to the unchanging task, and the settlements took their growth after a way of their own.

The Albemarle settlers, whose region presently came to be called "North" Carolina, were, on the whole, the more indulged. They endured many things, it is true, of many governors,—even to open robbery at the hands of one Seth Sothel, who bought the Earl of Clarendon's interest in the colony and came among them to rule as proprietor and get what he could out of his purchase on the spot. But they drove him from the colony in 1689, after having put up with his intolerable insolence and greed for five years together with more than their ordinary patience. They made their temper pretty clearly understood at last, and were suffered to go their own way in most things, with only enough interference and enough demands for quit-rents to keep them uncomfortably in mind of the proprietors. The settlements about the broad Sound slowly filled, and were not a little steadied in their ways of life by a constant increase in the number of Quakers among them. French Protestants came also, and made settlements of their own a little farther to the southward, in Pamlico and on the Neuse and Trent. Swiss and Germans founded a little hamlet at New Berne. The rich heart of the fertile country within was still untouched. There were barely five thousand people there in the year 1700, after forty years of growth. The proprietors had little to show thereabout for their ambitious efforts at colony building. But the colonists themselves took heart to believe their lot established, and no one could doubt that here were at least communities about whose maintenance there need be no concern. They were there to stay, and to grow, though it were never so slowly.

There was more to be seen at the other far-away settlements in "South" Carolina,—a town, at any rate, and a safe port of entry, such as there was not anywhere upon the northern sounds. Charleston had been removed in

ORIGINAL BROAD SEAL OF SOUTH CAROLINA

1680 from its first site to a fine point of land which lay opposite, where the Ashley and Cooper rivers joined to make a spacious harbor before passing to the sea. The removal had proved a mere stage in its growth,—a proof of its vitality. Englishmen, Irishmen, Scotsmen. Frenchmen, Germans sought the new colony out and made their several contributions to its founding. But the proprietors reaped little benefit. The English and Scottish colonists were not easy men to deal with when governors put the interests of the proprietors before the interests of the colony, or insisted, as they were bidden to insist, upon the enforcement of the impossible Fundamental Constitutions. Moreover, there were troubles peculiar to the place. The Spanish were close at hand at St. Augustine, watching their chance to attack and destroy the settlement. The colonists invited danger of still another kind by seizing Indians for slaves, and so exasperating the redskins. The English-speaking colonists did not wish to admit the Frenchmen who came among them to the full privileges upon which they insisted for themselves; but they were very keen for their own rights, and understood very well to what they were entitled under the charter to the proprietors. Governors lived no more comfortably among them than among the people of North Carolina. There were twenty-five hundred settlers in the colony by the time the new Charleston at the confluence of the rivers was six years old (1686), and seven thousand by the time the century was out (1700); but the more numerous they grew, the more steadfastly did they insist upon having no government they did not like.

Proprietary government was proving quite as difficult, meanwhile, in New Jersey; but the monotony of failure had been broken there by the sudden re-entry of the Dutch upon the scene. England and France had joined in war against Holland in 1672, and a hostile Dutch fleet presently found its way to the coasts of America. It first preyed upon the commerce of Virginia and Maryland in the south, and then, standing to the northward, entered the familiar harbor at New York, and took possession as easily as Colonel Nicolls had taken possession nine years before. From August, 1673, to November, 1674, the Dutch were masters in their old seats; there was no New York, no New Jersey; all alike was New Netherland once more. But it was a mere episode, a mere passing reminder of the old days when the Dutch were really masters there. In 1674 the war ended, and England regained her provinces by the treaty of peace (Treaty of Westminster, February 9, 1674).

SIR EDMUND ANDROS

The withdrawal of the Dutch, however, did not put the affairs of the English back at the point at which they had been broken off by the conquest. There were new difficulties to face. Philip Carteret again became governor in New Jersey, for Sir George Carteret, the proprietor; and for a little his task seemed easier than it had been before the Dutch came. The chief English towns of the province had stubbornly resisted his authority until the very eve of the coming of the Dutch men-of-war, though he had been steadfast and had not ceased to rule in such matters as he could, or to press the interests and the powers of the proprietor. At last documents had come out of England which conclusively put an end to the claim of the uneasy colonists that they had a right to act independently of the proprietor; but they had hardly reached Carteret before the Dutch fleet came in. When the Dutch were gone again the once discontented towns received their English governor back with a sort of satisfaction, having been gladdened to see the alien masters go. But there were new difficulties, because Edmund Andros, that stirring major of dragoons, was governor of New York. King Charles made a new grant of New York to his brother the Duke of York in 1674, to cure any doubt the Dutch occupation might be thought to have put upon his title; and the Duke promptly granted East New Jersey over again to Sir George Carteret; but the new grant was not couched in the terms of the old, left a doubt upon the mind of a careful reader whether it meant to renew Sir George's sovereignty or only Sir George's ownership as overlord,—and his Grace had explicitly commissioned Andros to be his deputy in the government of New York "and its dependencies." Andros understood Carteret's new charter literally, as it read, and acted as if he had been bidden annul the right of Sir George's governor to govern. He saw to it that the New Jersey towns should get as little comfort

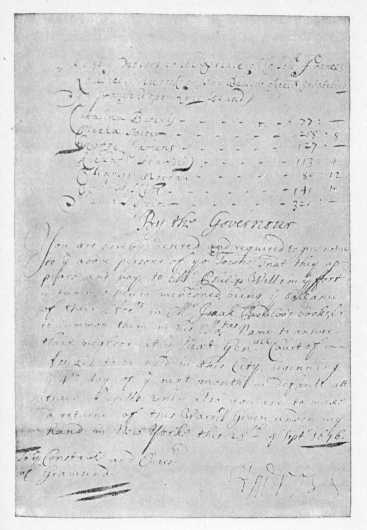

DOCUMENT BEARING AUTOGRAPH OF SIR EDMUND ANDROS

out of the resumption of their separate government as possible. He was a bluff soldier, bred in the school of Prince Rupert, as honest as he was direct and determined,—not a man to originate a policy of his own, but sure to do what he understood he was commanded to do very absolutely, without tact or scruple or hesitation, with the rough energy of a man who was no politician, but only a soldier. Moreover, he had in him the warm blood of thirty-four. At first he contented himself with collecting customs duties at the New Jersey ports as well as at New York for the Duke's revenues; but when Sir George Carteret died, in January, 1680, he went further. He challenged Philip Carteret's authority outright, accused him of acting without legal warrant within the Duke of York's patent, "to the great disturbance of his Majesty's subjects," and, when he would not yield, seized him, deposed him from his government by force, and himself assumed the authority of governor in the New Jersey towns. The next year, 1681, saw Carteret upheld and reinstated and Andros rebuked by official letters out of England, and the discredited soldier went home to give his account of the affair. East Jersey was to have quiet again for a little under new proprietors.

The King's new grants made of New Jersey, not a single province, as before, but two distinct provinces, East Jersey and West Jersey. Lord Berkeley, Sir George Carteret's associate in the original grant, had sold his interest in the province early in 1673, before the Dutch came, and when the Dutch were gone again Sir George Carteret's grant was renewed, not for the whole of New Jersey, but only for "East" Jersey. "West" Jersey passed into the hands of those who had bought out Lord

Berkeley's interest in the original gift. It included all the southwestern portion of the province, below a line drawn from Little Egg Harbor at the sea sharply north and northwest to the northernmost branch of the Delaware in latitude 40° 41′. Its lands lay upon the great river from end to end, almost, of the original grant. All the spreading waters of the stream below and of the great Bay through which it opened to the sea were its highway and frontier.

East Jersey passed, after Sir George Carteret's death, to a numerous company of proprietors, by purchase (1681),—men of all "religions, professions, and characters." Some were high prerogative men, likely to be of any king's party; some were dissenters, some papists, some Quakers. The governors whom they sent out were not likely to push any one interest or opinion or scheme of authority, and their province fell upon quieter days, when governors and colonists could generally agree and live in peace together.

West Jersey seemed sometimes, to outsiders, a place with no government at all. It, too, had numerous proprietors, whose shares were constantly changing hands, to the confusion both of questions of ownership and questions of government. But there was, in fact, a quiet growth of prosperous settlements, nevertheless. The several hamlets planted within the little province were established by people abundantly able to take care of themselves, and local government went peacefully on, whether there was any definite guiding authority fixed for the colony as a whole or not. Moreover, there was in due time, when affairs had settled and taken on a normal face, a very well ordered government for the province, under a popular assembly to which the proprietors accorded powers very freely, and which they let their governors heed and obey in a way that other colonies might very well have envied.

Both provinces prospered. Many settlers preferred the Jerseys to New York. There was less taxation there, and less interference with merchants' dealings. The currency was kept freer from sudden changes of value than elsewhere, because the law did not play with its value. In West Jersey the laws for the punishment and suppression of crime were singularly humane and just. A wilderness lay between the towns near New York and on the Monmouth grant and the towns upon the Delaware; only an Indian trail here and there, like that which ran from the Puritan settlement at Newark south and southwest to the river, threaded the untouched forests; and it was not easy to pass from the one region to the other except by sea. But settlers poured in very steadily to the parts that were open, from New England and Long Island especially, as well as from over sea. Saw mills and iron mills were set up; tar, pitch, and turpentine were shipped in paying quantities from the pine forests; whales, caught upon the very coasts, yielded rich supplies of oil and whalebone; and the Jerseys made ready to be as forward as any other colony in growth and self-support.

The democratic government of West Jersey, the humane clemency of its laws, the full freedom of religious belief allowed to all comers, and all the features of liberality and tolerance which drew settlers to the Delaware were due in no small degree to the presence of influential Quakers among its proprietors. Among the rest was William Penn, a man at whose hands schemes of proprietorship in America were to receive a

WILLIAM PENN

new dignity, and a touch almost of romance. He was but thirty-one when he bought a share in the province of West Jersey (1675). He had been born in 1644, the year before Mr. Ingle turned reformer and roving governor in Maryland,—two years after Sir William Berkeley came out to be governor in Virginia. That was

WILLIAM PENN'S FIRST RESIDENCE IN AMERICA (LETITIA COTTAGE)

also the year in which Mr. George Fox, the founder of the sect of Quakers, first began, a lad of twenty, to preach a new way of life. He preached no new creed, but only simplicity and purity of life, the direct gift of a guiding light from Heaven, without intermediation of priest or church or learned dogma, the independence of every man's conscience, and his freedom from the authority of man or government in such things as concerned the life of the spirit. He spoke such words as made men's hearts burn within them, and quickly kindled a fire which no man could put out or check. William Penn had become his follower at twenty-four, taken captive almost upon a first hearing by the new and generous way of thought which so gently bade men better their lives.

Penn was singularly unlike the plain, unlettered people who had been the first to hear Mr. Fox with glad-

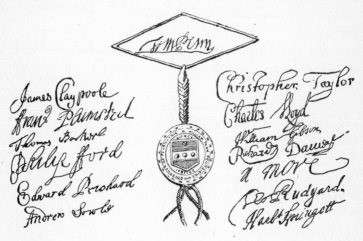

SEAL AND SIGNATURES OF THE PENNSYLVANIA FRAME OF GOVERNMENT

ness and live as he counselled. He was son to Sir William Penn, whom all the world knew as admiral in the royal navy, a great career behind him, a favorite with the King for the service he had done him when he was restored,—half man of the world, half bluff sailor; a man of fortune, and of a direct and ready fashion of making his own way; no lover of new-fangled notions or young men's whims; and his son had so handsome a person, so gallant a manner, so manifest a charm in what he said and did, that Sir William's head was filled with dreams of what he should become,—dreams of preferment and a notable career in affairs. It astounded and angered him mightily that the boy should turn Quaker and give up everything for a set of foolish notions. But it half pleased the old man, after all, when his first choler was passed, to see how steadfast his son was. It half amused him to recognize his own wilfulness turned to such a use. Presently he forgave the strange lad, like the frank sailor he was, and helped him to succeed in another way.

THE PENN ARMS

And so it turned out that West Jersey was bought,—so far as Mr. Penn and those who thought with him among the new proprietors were concerned,—to be a refuge and place of peace for the Quakers. It was the Quakers who principally crowded into the new province and gave it its prosperity and its sober way in affairs. But Mr. Penn's plans widened as his thought became engaged in this great matter. A mere share in the ownership of West Jersey did not satisfy him. He determined to have a province of his own, a Quaker colony upon a great scale. The outcome of that purpose was the founding of Pennsylvania, whose peaceful story of orderly government and quick prosperity reads like the incidents, almost, of an idyl amidst the confused annals of colonial affairs in that day of change. Sir William Penn had died in 1670, and had left to his son, among other items of an ample fortune, a claim for sixteen thousand pounds against the crown. The young Quaker asked for a grant of land in America in satisfaction of the claim, and the King readily enough consented, glad to please an old friend's son and be quit of an obligation so easily. Penn asked for and obtained the land "lying north of Maryland, on the east bounded with Delaware River, on the west limited as Maryland is, and northward to extend as far as plantable" into the unclaimed Indian country; and the King pleased his own fancy by calling the grant "Pennsylvania," in honor of the old admiral whose claim against the crown he was thus paying off. The grant was dated March 4, 1681.

SEAL OF MASSACHUSETTS PROVINCE

There was a charming frankness and nobility about the spirit in which the young proprietor set out upon his great enterprise. He admitted "that government was a business he had never undertaken," but he promptly assured those who were already settled in his province that they should be "at the mercy of no governor who comes to make his fortune great. You shall be governed by laws of your own making," he said, "and live a free and, if you will, a sober and industrious people." "For the matter of liberty and privilege," he declared, "I propose that which is extraordinary, and to leave myself and successors no power of doing mischief,—that the will of one may not hinder the good of a whole country." His wish was to honor God and the principles of the despised sect in whose service he had embarked his faith and his fortune. "The nations want a precedent," he said; and it was his hope to give it them as boldly

and wisely as possible. It was his belief, as it was
the belief of the great Edmund Burke a hundred
years afterwards, "that any government is free to
the people under it (whatever be the frame) where the
laws rule and the people are a party to those laws."
He meant that his colonists should have such freedom
as his gift, and at the very beginning of their government.

There were, when he set up his gentle rule, scarcely
five hundred white men, all told, settled within the ter-

MASSACHUSETTS COINAGE

ritory Charles had given him: a few tiny Swedish hamlets, a few Quaker families who had crossed the river
from West Jersey, stragglers here and there, looking
for good lands. There was something of a village at
Upland (whose name Mr. Penn was presently to change
to Chester), on the river, where the authority of the new
proprietor was first proclaimed and his liberal plan of
government made known in September, 1681; but the
real creation of the colony was to follow, when colonists
began to pour in under the new arrangement. In August, 1682, Mr. Penn added to his first grant from the

King the lands lying about New Castle and below, by purchase from the Duke of York, to whom they had passed with the rest of New Netherland when the Dutch were ousted; and a few hundred more were thereby added to the number of his colonists, Dutch as well as Swedes, and a few score scattered groups of lonely settlers. Maryland hotly protested the new grant. Her own charter gave her the Delaware for eastern boundary. She had never acknowledged the title of the Dutch there, and thought the title of his Grace of York no better. But her protests were not heeded. Mr. Penn was determined not to be shut within the continent, but to get his own outlet to the sea, and took what the wilful Stuart granted him. The very month of that new grant, August, 1682, he himself took ship for his province, with a goodly company of Quakers, to begin the real planting of the new region. He reached the colony in October; and during that autumn and the winter which followed (1682–1683) no fewer than twenty - three ships came into the Delaware bringing immigrants; to be followed presently by other ships seeking trade.

Within but a little more than a single year of his coming, Mr. Penn could boast, "I have led the greatest colony into America that ever any man did upon a private credit, and the most prosperous beginnings that ever were in it are to be found among us." By 1685 there were more than seven thousand settlers there. Englishmen predominated among them, but almost one-half the number were of other nationalities,—French, Dutch, Swedes, Germans, Finns, Scots-Irishmen, whoever would come, men of all creeds and kinds, who had sought out the free place and had been accorded an ungrudging welcome. A company of Welsh Quakers arrived before the proprietor himself (August, 1682), and settled upon a tract apart, which it had been agreed beforehand they should have. The next year came a little colony of Germans to obtain like privileges upon a grant of their own, and to make ready for others of their race, a great many, who were to follow. And so company followed company, now of one nationality and again of another, bringing what creed and what peace-

PROVINCE HOUSE, RESIDENCE OF THE ROYAL GOVERNORS OF MASSACHUSETTS

ful practices of self-government they pleased, to be received and given grants of land without question. Quakers for a while predominated, as Mr. Penn had wished. The German settlers were most of them Mennonites, whose creed and way of simple living were very like those Mr. Fox had preached. And where there were Quakers government was apt to be a very simple matter. Few officers were needed in their hamlets, and for a while no courts at all. They settled their common affairs not only, but the private quarrels, differences, and difficulties of their members also, very quietly in their own stated meetings, and seemed to know the secret of enforcing good temper as well as orderly conduct in a way very honorable to their principles.

The chief town of the province was established at the confluence of the two fine rivers Delaware and Schuylkill, and Mr. Penn named it Philadelphia, wishing it to be a place of peace and good-will. At first those who were to build there lived in caves cut out of the bluffs which lined the river; but they were quick at substitut-

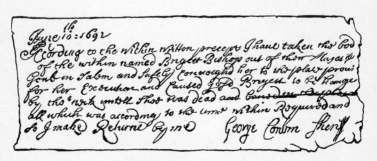

FACSIMILE OF A SHERIFF'S RETURN EXECUTION OF A WITCH

ing good houses. By the end of the year 1683 there were no fewer than one hundred and fifty dwellings built,—frail and cheap enough, no doubt, but sufficient until stone and brick could be had, and time in which to build with them. The change came very soon. The sober, substantial, yeomanlike folk who came into the colony preferred, whenever it was possible, to build of good, lasting stuff, and to build solidly and well. Before Mr. Penn sailed for home, in 1684, there were already three hundred and fifty houses erected, some of them several stories high, built with cellars and decorated with balconies. Outside the central town, with

A PENNSYLVANIA CAVE-DWELLING IN 1683

its busy two thousand colonists, there were quite fifty hamlets in the thriving province.

Government did not go quite so easily after Mr. Penn returned to England. He left men behind who wished to have their own way, and whom no authority less than his own could restrain. "For the love of God, me, and the poor country," he wrote them, "be not so *governmentish*, so uneasy and open in your dissatisfaction." But, though the growth and prosperity of the colony were a little retarded by the bickerings of those left in control, there was, after all, less turbulence in the sober colony than Pennsylvania's neighbor settlements had made shift to put up with and survive. The government was liberal in all things, and very simple in its make-up, — upon the familiar model of deputy governor, council, and assembly. The courts did not attempt the elaborate procedure of the courts at home. There were not lawyers enough in the colony for that, and no one was very anxious to see more of them there. A very simple method of trial sufficed for simple causes, with or without juries as the parties to the suit might agree; and the Quakers at their periodical meetings saw to it that as few of their own people should resort to the courts as possible. That various population was of course too heterogeneous and too spirited not to give its rulers trouble; but it went on to prosper very well, and to make its way in the world in a fashion so orderly that its neighbors might well have looked on in envious wonder.

For one thing, it kept peace with the Indians as its neighbors could not. The Quakers everywhere seemed to win the confidence of the redmen upon the instant, as Roger Williams had won it, whose doctrines and principles of life were so like their own. They won it by loving justice and keeping faith, and Mr. Penn set them an example which neither they nor any others who heard of it were likely to forget. He scrupulously

PAGE OF TUNES FROM THE "BAY PSALM BOOK"

purchased the land he occupied of its native owners. He hoped for their speedy civilization, and stipulated in the contracts which he made with those who in turn purchased from him that the Indians should have "the same liberties to improve their grounds and provide for the sustenance of their families as the planters"

who were established there.   There was something that
took hold of men's imaginations in the sober conference
he held with the Indians, as if with the leaders of an
equal race, at Shackamaxon, June 23, 1683, and in
the terms of the free treaty then entered into.   Peace
between the white men and the red in Pennsylvania
rested always upon the firm foundations of mutual
confidence which were laid that day.   It was a peace
whose guarantee was good-will and friendliness.   It
was a colony of rigorous laws.   "Profanity, drunken-
ness, the drinking of healths, duelling, stage plays,
masks, revels, bull-baiting, cock-fighting, cards, dice,
and lotteries were all prohibited," and women might be
fined for clamorous scolding, quite as in Puritan New
England.   But it was a more kindly rigor, as the Indians perceived.   The New Englanders had sought to be
just with the redmen; but the Quakers sought to add a
gentle kindliness to justice, and their peace was more
lasting than that of the English in the north.

And yet not even their fine temper and quick spirit
of justice could have so steadily held the restless redskins off from mischief had not the fates of the forest
made their borders a place of peace.   The Indians they
dealt with were not the men who had once made that
wilderness a place of dread and caution.   Six years
before Mr. Penn got his charter (1675) the formidable
Susquehannocks, once masters there, had turned their
faces to the south, beaten and in retreat before the implacable hatred of their kinsmen of the Five Nations at
the north, and had gone to harry the borders of Maryland
and Virginia and bring Mr. Bacon to his fate.   There
were now none but humble Delawares to be dealt with
in Mr. Penn's province, men who paid their tribute

right promptly to the masterful Iroquois who had driven the Susquehannocks out, accepted them as masters, and dared not lift a hand against the English, whom the Iroquois received and fought for as friends and allies.

The next year after Mr. Penn's meeting with the Indians at Shackamaxon saw an infinitely more important treaty concluded with the Indians in the north. This was the treaty made with the great Iroquois confederacy itself at Albany, on the 2d of August, 1684, to secure the frontiers of the English alike against the redmen and against the French. The tribes of that memorable confederacy were the most capable and formidable anywhere to be found upon the eastern stretches of the continent. Their power extended from the lakes to the borders of the Carolina grant,—as the Susquehannocks had reason to know. The Dutch in New Netherland had early won their friendship,—the French in Canada their bitter enmity. It was with the firearms the Dutch had sold them that they had made themselves masters in all the Indian country north and south, and had brought their power to such a pitch that no settlement of the white man was safe without their good-will. The French had long ago sent missionaries among them, to speak to them both of the true God and of the sacred authority of his Majesty their king in France, and had used, through these, every argument of interest and every threat of power to bring them to an alliance; but the shrewd sachems who were their statesmen had stood out unchangingly against their advances, and had held fast to the English, seeing very clearly in their calm counsels, as they sat apart, how much greater the power of the

AT AN IROQUOIS COUNCIL FIRE

white men grew in the south than in the north. The English governors of New York were as quick as the Dutch rulers of New Netherland had been to see the priceless value of this protecting friendship of the border, no less than of the great trade in furs of which it made Albany the mart and centre. They saw how it would serve them when it should come to the final rivalry between French and English for the possession of the interior of the continent; and they held the French off by a very close alliance with the masters of the forests.

Governor Andros, being a soldier and man of affairs, had seen to this critical matter in person, going himself to the stronghold of the Mohawks and establishing a permanent board of Indian commissioners to keep warm the alliance with the powerful confederacy which the Mohawks represented. He was as efficient in the proper affairs of his own province of New York as he was arbitrary in pushing for authority beyond its borders in the Jerseys. And Colonel Thomas Dongan, whom the Duke of York selected to succeed him in the government of the colony, was no less watchful and competent. Had his Grace known as well how to choose servants and counsellors in England, he had fared better, and might have kept his throne when he came to it. Colonel Dongan was a soldier, an Irishman, and a Roman Catholic, and had served in the armies of France,—no good school for an English governor, — and yet he proved himself a wise ruler in a colony in which the Duke, his master, saw fit to permit liberty of conscience and to observe a very liberal policy in affairs.

Colonel Nicolls had established a singular government in New York at the very outset, nineteen years ago. There was nobody in all its organization to represent the colonists. Its officers were appointed; its decrees were absolute. But its decrees were also liberal and just, made in the interest of the colony as well as in the interest of the Duke. Andros had been knighted for his services there, and was Sir Edmund when he went home in 1681 to explain his quarrel with Philip Carteret; and no wonder, for he had done a notable

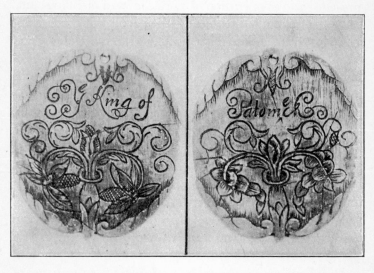

MEDAL PRESENTED BY JAMES II. TO THE KING OF THE POTOMACKS

thing. He had strictly enforced the laws of trade, admitting no vessel to discharge her cargo at the great bay where his government was which had not paid duties or made clearances as the English statutes commanded; and, instead of breeding rebellion by what he did, had linked New York to the home ports in England by a direct trade across sea, which every year grew greater, and which steadily tended to make his province the chief home in all America of loyalty and cordial feeling for the mother country, a chief port of entry for English ideas and English sympathies.

Colonel Dongan did no less for the Duke's authority, but in another way. In his treaty with the Indians, that notable treaty of August, 1684, he did no more than confirm the policy of Sir Edmund and the Dutch. What made the treaty so impressive an event was the presence and co-operation of Lord Howard of Effingham, now governor of Virginia. It was an agreement establishing not merely the safety of the borders of New York, but also the claim of the English to a sort of sovereignty and overlordship over all the great stretches of the continent south and southwest of Lake Ontario. It concerned Virginia no less than it concerned New York; and the redskins regarded it the more because of the presence of the ruler of the English in far-away Virginia, as well as of the Duke's governor in New York.

Colonel Dongan had been instructed to play a very different *rôle* in the internal government of his province from that which Andros had played. Despite the very liberal measures adopted and the sound public spirit shown by the Duke's governors hitherto, it was not in English nature to be satisfied for twenty years together without such an assembly to speak and act for the people as every other colony had, north and south. Emphatic protests and a strong appeal crossed the sea close upon the heels of Sir Edmund Andros in 1681,—speaking not so much discontent with the Duke's governor as a firm and rooted objection to the form of government, which the colony now seemed entitled to say that it had outgrown; and the Duke thought it wise to yield. Colonel Dongan came, in August, 1683, instructed to appoint a council and call an assembly;

317

and by October New York had a government like that of her neighbor colonies. No tax or imposition was to be laid or law made except by act of assembly,—and that looked like privilege enough. The new governor, too, might well be to the mind of all who liked candor and capacity. He had the blithe humor of his race, and was a man to approve and relish as a comrade; and yet his firm purpose and clear eye in all points of action made him also a man to respect, obey, and follow.

And then, when all things seemed settled, of a sudden the whole sky changed, because in February, 1685, Charles II. died, and the Duke reigned in his stead, as James II.,—a man whom all the world knew to be a Roman Catholic, and presently discovered to be a tyrant, the more intolerable for his solemn bigotry. The same year Louis XIV., king in France, revoked the great Edict of Nantes, forbade the Protestants their worship in his kingdom, and so drove fifty thousand of the best people of France,—soldiers, men of letters, craftsmen, artificers,—forth from the land they had enriched, to make Holland, England, Brandenburg, and America so much the better off for their skill and thrifty industry. By spring-time Monmouth and Argyle were in the field, and England saw rebellion lift its head again, both in Scotland and in the south. It was an ominous beginning for the sullen King; and the colonies were to get their share of the change which his reign brought to Englishmen everywhere.

It was a brief reign enough. James ran his course of tyranny with a sort of bitter haste, and had finished the mad business before the fourth year of his rule was ended. The first year (1685) saw the brutal Jeffreys ride his bloody circuit through Somerset and Dorset,

New York December 13 1683

Sr

I give you my hearty sincere thanks for your kind Entertainment I am afraid this winter season will not give me leave to see my good friend in your Province and I very much wish for an opportunity to do it. there is no one more resolved and fixt, to demonstrate himselfe, ready to do all offices, of friendshipp, then I am being very much obliged by you, to doe so, I have written to his Royall highness, & tho as much as I could in your commendation yet farr short of yr Character you meritt. this messenger stays, & I have no longer time, then to assure you of my unfeigned services, & Respects, and that I am Effectively

Sr
Your most Humble & affectionate servt

Tho Dongan

ffor
Governr Penn
Pennsylvania

Capt Talbott is going away to morrow morning

LETTER OF DONGAN TO WILLIAM PENN

to hang, scourge, or behead those who had incurred suspicion of sympathy, were it never so remote or slight, with Monmouth's rising. More than eight hundred persons were sold into slavery over sea; three hundred and fifty said to be rebels were hanged; women were scourged from market-town to market-town, sent to the block, or burned; and all England stood horror-stricken to see the King's revenge and bitter hate. The next year saw him openly bent upon freeing the Romish Church by his own authority from all restraint of law. Statutes he set aside by the use of what he said was the crown's prerogative. He declared all creeds free; but he forbade the ministers of the established Church to preach its Protestant doctrine. Bishops who would not yield to his will he haled before the courts; and, lest the ordinary courts should prove disobedient, he set up a special Court of Ecclesiastical Commission, to do what he should bid in the discipline of the Church. He maintained a standing army without the consent or vote of Parliament, and levied taxes without its authorization. He was as subservient to France as to the Church of Rome, and admitted no one to his counsels who would not accept his creed and do his bidding.

It was strange the nation held its hand so long; and yet the end came swiftly enough. By midsummer, 1688, those who were ready to risk their lives and fortunes for England's constitution had urgently prayed William, Prince of Orange, to come into England, put James from his throne, and save their liberties. William was husband to Mary, James's daughter; was a Protestant, a statesman, and a man of honor. He came with an army at his back. But it was not necessary to conquer England. She knew her straits and was ready and glad to receive him. James miserably fled; the Parliament accepted his flight as a voluntary abdication; and the throne went by act of Parliament to William and Mary. Thus was accomplished what

James. JAMES II.

men who loved the ancient liberties of England were afterwards to look back to as "the glorious Revolution of 1688." No king should henceforth pretend to any right to rule without consent of the Parliament, or in despite of the liberties of the nation which had executed Charles, ousted James, and re-established the throne in such fashion as suited its sense of justice and its own security. It was the formal setting up, as public law of England, of the bold doctrine of the people's rights which Sir Edwin Sandys had preached from his place in the Commons seventy-six years ago to the deep displeasing of James I. The momentous thing was over and complete by February, 1689; and it was then just four years since Charles II. died.

For the northern colonies in America those four years had meant a memorable change of government, as ill to live under, almost, as the tyranny in England. For a little while after the loss of her charter in 1684 affairs had moved on smoothly and without serious incident in Massachusetts, though half-heartedly enough, it was plain, under a provisional government, waiting to see what the crown would do. The death of King Charles delayed a settlement; but James, when he came to the throne, very promptly showed what he meant to do. He resolved to put Massachusetts and the colonies lying immediately about her into the hands of a royal governor and an appointed council, without an assembly or any other arrangement for a participation of the people in the management of their affairs. At first (May, 1686) he named Joseph Dudley "President of the Council for Massachusetts Bay, New Hampshire, and Maine, and the Narragansett country, or King's Province," but gave him no authority to alter law or impose taxes. But that was only a temporary arrangement. The real change came with the arrival of Sir Edmund Andros, in December, 1686, to be "Governor-General and Vice-Admiral"; and Plymouth was added to his government.

WILLIAM III.

Joseph Dudley had been unwelcome enough. It was a bitter thing for the people of Massachusetts to have this man, whom they deemed a traitor, nothing less, set over them. He was the son of Thomas Dudley, the stern Puritan of their day of first exile and settlement, who had been second to great Winthrop in the founding of the colony. And now Thomas Dudley's son, once their agent in London to defend their charter, had consented to serve the crown in the overthrow of their liberties. But Andros was worse. Dudley was at least timid and time-serving and doubtful of his power; but Sir Edmund came with instructions and with a temper of command which no one could mistake. He meant no rank injustice, indeed, but he was no statesman, knew only the rough way of the soldier in carrying out his instructions, and had very definite and unpalatable instructions to carry out. He was bidden appoint persons of the best character and estate to his council, and to disturb the existing law of the colonies as little as possible; but he was also commanded to allow no printing press within his jurisdiction; to insist upon a universal toleration in matters of religion,—especially upon the encouragement of the worship of the Church of England; and to execute with vigilance and vigor the laws of trade. He was given, too, a small number of royal troops for his support, whose red coats were sadly unwelcome in Boston. Worst of all, he was authorized to govern and to lay taxes without an assembly.

This was evidently the sort of government the King meant to set up everywhere in the colonies. He had instructed the officers of the crown almost at the very outset of his reign to secure the annulment of the other colonial charters, and suits had already been prosecuted in the courts against Connecticut and Rhode Island, against the Carolina grants, and even against those he had himself given only the other day in New Jersey.

A NEW
VOYAGE
TO
CAROLINA;

CONTAINING THE

Exact Description and *Natural History*

OF THAT

COUNTRY:

Together with the *Present State* thereof.

AND

A JOURNAL

Of a Thousand Miles, Travel'd thro' several
Nations of *INDIANS*.

Giving a particular Account of their Customs,
Manners, *&c.*

By JOHN LAWSON, Gent. Surveyor-
General of *North-Carolina*.

LONDON:

Printed in the Year 1709.

TITLE-PAGE OF LAWSON'S "A NEW VOYAGE TO CAROLINA"

The next year after Andros's coming (1687) he turned upon Maryland. New York and Virginia were already practically his own, to deal with as he pleased. The same year Andros went to Boston, Governor Dongan, of New York, was instructed to forbid the popular assemblies granted but three years before. He was commanded, too, as Andros was, "to allow no printing press." James meant to be master everywhere, and to permit not so much as a word of public comment upon what his servants did; and all America felt the change. Before the first month of his administration was over, Andros, acting upon the King's command, had dissolved the government of Rhode Island, and assumed control of its affairs. The next year he did the same in Connecticut; and in 1688 New York and the Jerseys were nominally added to his government, Francis Nicholson acting as his deputy there.

The chief general *authorities* for the history of Pennsylvania during the seventeenth century and the first years of the eighteenth are the second volumes of Bancroft and Hildreth ; the second volume of Bryant and Gay's *Popular History of the United States ;* John Fiske's *Dutch and Quaker Colonies ;* F. D. Stone's *The Founding of Pennsylvania,* in the third volume of Winsor's *Narrative and Critical History of America ;* S. M. Janney's *Life of William Penn ;* C. B. Keen's *New Sweden, or the Swedes on the Delaware,* in the fourth volume of Winsor ; Thomas F. Gordon's *History of Pennsylvania from its Discovery by Europeans to 1776 ;* Samuel Hazard's *Annals of Pennsylvania from the Discovery of the Delaware, 1609-1682 ;* and Robert Proud's *History of Pennsylvania from the Original Settlement in 1681 till after the Year 1742.*

The chief *sources* are to be found in Samuel Hazard's *Pennsylvania Archives ; Minutes of the Provincial Council of Pennsylvania; Colonial Records of Pennsylvania ; Duke of Yorke's Book of Laws* (1676–1682) and *Charter to William Penn and Laws of the Province of Pennsylvania passed between 1682 and 1700,* compiled by Staughton George and others; *Votes and Proceed-*

ings of the House of Representatives of the Province of Pennsylvania ; *Memoirs* of the Pennsylvania Historical Society ; Ben Perley Poore's *The Federal and State Constitutions, Colonial Charters, and other Organic Laws of the United States ; The Pennsylvania Magazine of History and Biography ;* and Stedman and Hutchinson's *Library of American Literature.*

HAPPILY the new tyranny had no longer life in America than in England. It came promptly enough to its end when the news reached the colonies of James's disgrace and flight and William's coming. The Boston people rose, as if by a common instinct; seized Andros and his officers; seized the fort; seized even the King's frigate lying in the harbor; and resumed their old government under their old magistrates, to await further tidings from over sea. The other colonies round about followed suit. Sir Edmund had got himself well hated. He was an honest, well-meaning man enough, a plain and not very quick-witted soldier who executed his orders quite literally; but he was arbitrary and harsh, and showed sometimes an unwise and ugly temper when he was opposed. And the orders he tried to execute were intolerable to the people of the once free colony he governed. He levied taxes by the authority of the crown; he demanded quit-rents of all the land owners of the colony, because the loss of the charter, he was told by the law officers in England, destroyed the right of the colonists to the land they had acquired under it; he forbade even the ordinary town meetings; and he sought to crush opposition by harsh punishments. To these Puritans it was no small part of the trying experience that he encouraged some to set up a society to worship after the manner of the Church of England, and use

328

the hated prayer-book; and that in 1688 the Episcopal congregation thus formed built a place of worship, which they called King's Chapel, in Boston. It was a happy day when they got rid of the hateful tyranny; and an assurance of better times when they presently learned that the new government at home approved what they had done, and were willing that they should send Sir Edmund and his fellow prisoners to England for trial.

The action of the people was no less prompt and decisive in New York, James's own province. Francis Nicholson, Andros's deputy in New York and the Jerseys, was as little liked there as Andros himself was in Boston. Both he and the members of his council, because they supported him, were looked upon as tools of a papist king, and New York was Dutch and Protestant. The two regiments of the King's regulars Sir Edmund had brought with him upon his second coming out, to be governor of all the northern coast, were Irish Catholics every man, and Nicholson had come out as commander of one of them. To the uneasy suspicions of the critical Protestants of the little seaport, affairs wore the ugly look of having brought them into the power of men who must of necessity prove the enemies of a Protestant king. With news of the revolution in England, moreover, came also news of war with France, the ousted King's Romish friend and ally; and the King's officers fell into an evident panic. While they hesitated what to do, a captain of the men-at-arms they had called together for their defence seized the fort and the government in the name of the Prince of Orange. This was Jacob Leisler. He had come to the colony close upon thirty years before (1660), as a soldier in the employ of the Dutch West India Company;

New-England's Spirit of Persecution

Transmitted To

PENNSILVANIA,

And the Pretended *Quaker* found Persecuting the True

Chriſtian - Quaker,

IN THE

TRYAL

OF

Peter Boſs, George Keith, Thomas Budd,
and *William Bradford,*

At the Seſſions held at *Philadelphia* the Nineth, Tenth and
Twelfth Days of *December*, 1692. Giving an Account
of the moſt Arbitrary Procedure of that Court,

Printed in the Year 1693.

had thriven in trade and made a place of influence for himself among the colonists; and now stepped forth as their champion against the officers of the papist King whom the Parliament had deposed.

It was the news of war that chiefly wrought upon the fears of the town. It was yet spring-time, 1689, and the news that war had actually begun reached New York, a hasty rumor, before the fact. But it spoke truth, nevertheless; and no man could be ignorant what special interest New York had in the matter. Louis of France was in fact planning that very spring how he should make the place his own, to the undoing of the English in America. With the coming of summer his plans were complete. The veteran, indomitable Frontenac, master, if any man was, of the strategy of the forest, was to go back to Canada to take a force of one thousand French regulars and six hundred Canadians through the northern wilderness to Albany, thence to sweep down the river and meet the King's fleet, sent timely out of France, at New York; and France was to be mistress at the centre of the continent before another winter was out, ready to strike a final blow, first at the Iroquois behind her in the forests, and then at the English on the northern coasts. France made no sign as yet; the whole plan kept covert in Paris, a closely guarded secret; no one in America knew what was afoot. But some seemed able to divine. A keen foreboding quickened the faculties of all who thought upon the hazard of fortunes in the struggle that had all but come; the air seemed full of something, — who could tell what?—and rumors crept through the forests and along the coasts in which men seemed to guess what Louis planned.

A̅ 1692 13 decemb̄ ... N: Yorke

A̅: Trew and pfect. Jnvantory off all the Good Catle
in Chatels yt appered to vs off M.r Sam: Leete Late dead
appraised according to orders of Court by Jacob Leisler
and M.r Paulus Richard and is as followeth 21

one feather bed Bolster and tvo pillowes vnder   04-15-00
rugg three blanketts on bedsted mat and furtins
Item Six Leether Chayres on Close Stoole and ... Chumbrpoth 02-05-0
Item on Smal trunck two Clath Coates and Breeches 02-00
Item on paire off trousers one gowne ffowre ffustion
Wastcoates   00-16-00
Item three Necloathes on paire of old towren Shirts 00-08-00
an handcherchiefe
Item three paire old black Stockings two paire old 00-08-00
thred one paire old wollen Stockings
Item three pare off false Sleeves two paire gloves 00-02-00
Item two Chests three Combes one knife on Small   00-16-00
botell in a Case
Item the bords on table for wrytengs   00-00-00
Item on table & the fellow not kin on howse
Glass one paire andirons on fier Shovell on paire 04-00-00
tostols on Carbine & on Sword
Item on old bridle and brest plate old Locks   00-04-00
with out keyes
Item on peice of Scheete lid one fate wth 13 botels 00-03-06
Item Thirty & printet boks grat and Small   05-16-00
Item on guilt bed and boulster and Six wooden   00-02-00
trenchers
Item on warming pan   00-10-00
Item all other things little and Lumbers not   00-00-00
named in ptiulars
                                                    4 "... 3 "... 0 "... 00

Paul Richard
Jacob Leisler

Not a few new-comers to the busy settlements which lay about the bay at New York had special reason to fear to see Louis strike. It was but four years since the revocation of the Edict of Nantes. Many a Huguenot family had found welcome there and a refuge from death, and knew not what fresh misfortune might overtake them should their insensate King take also these free coasts of the New World. Every rumor bred a deeper uneasiness. No ship came in at the Narrows which did not seem for a moment to be come out of France, no group of ships that did not look like a fleet of French frigates. Nothing was so easy as to throw the simpler people of the little town into a state of mind to be glad of any friendly leadership which seemed to make them safe against plotting Catholics, whether out of France or out of England. Leisler was sure of the sympathy of the crowd, and seemed to it to give proof of honesty in all that he did. As a matter of fact, there was no danger. Colonel Dongan had done his work too well in the diplomacy of the forest. He had won the Iroquois to an alliance of which they gave, that very summer, instant and timely proof. As if some English statesman had set their work for them, they made King Louis's plans impossible before ever they were put upon the field. Frontenac reached Canada in October to find that all the northern wilderness had been swept as with a flame by the fierce warriors of the great confederacy. The fur trade of the lakes was cut off; the posts upon the frontiers were taken and plundered; Montreal itself was barely saved from capture and destruction. There could be no expedition to Albany after that season's work of rapine and slaughter.

333

The
FRAME
OF THE
GOVERNMENT
Of the *Province* of
𝕻𝖊𝖓𝖓𝖘𝖞𝖑𝖛𝖆𝖓𝖎𝖆
In *America*.

Printed, and Sold by *Andrew Sowle* at
the Crooked-Billet in *Holloway-Lane* in
Shoreditch, 1691.

But New York did not know how safe it was; and Leisler had his day. It might have been well enough, had he stopped with thrusting Nicholson aside and assuming to play the new King's partisan and governor till the air should clear. But he did not. For a year and a half he maintained himself as governor, in the new King's name, but without his authority. He even resisted commissioned officers of the King, until a governor sent from England came; and then he was hanged for treason. It was a sad, unjust end. The man had been hot-headed, arbitrary, blind, and wilful, and had done much that the law could not sanction in order to have his own way; but he had done all, even that which was the deepest folly, in good faith. He had meant to serve the community he ruled, and had planned no treason against the King. There had been not a little of the heat of parties at the bottom of the trouble. The greater land owners, the King's officials, and the rich merchants had wished Nicholson to keep the government until the new King should send some one in his stead. The small tradesmen, the artisans, and the sailors of the town heard that there was war with France, and that a French fleet was coming against the place, and believed that the rich men and the officials among them were no lovers of common men's liberties, or of a Protestant church, either; and Leisler was their leader. His condemnation was a thing resolved upon and hurried to its execution in New York, not commanded from over sea; and in 1695 Parliament itself took off the stain of treason from his name.

In Maryland those who were unquiet and did not like the proprietor's government took advantage of the time to overthrow it. There were men enough who

GOVERNOR SLOUGHTER SIGNING THE DEATH WARRANT OF LEISLER

had watched for such a chance. Though discontent
with the proprietor's government had met very sharp
frustration and rebuke twelve years ago, when Davis
and Pate went to the gallows for the treason of emu-
lating the example of Mr. Bacon in Virginia, as many
wanted a change now as had wanted it then, and this
new opportunity seemed made for any who chose to act
upon its invitation. The mere fact of being governed
like a private estate and mediæval county palatine was
very irksome to the more ambitious spirits of the colony;
and the more closely and sedulously the proprietor
attended to his government the more irksome did it
become. He dealt very harshly with opposition; he
openly interfered with elections to the assembly; he
disallowed and set aside such legislation as he did not
like; he gave the offices of government to men of his
own kin or personal following; and the taxes were not
always spent for the public benefit. It was like the
government of Virginia with a petty king in residence.
And that petty king, every one knew, was of the popish
party, whose part the great King at home had played
to his own undoing. Men fancied they saw new popish
plots in every trivial incident or shifting of affairs.
If the panic had touched New York and turned her
government upside down, it was little to be wondered
at that it touched Maryland also. Richard Talbot,
Duke of Tyrconnel, the officer who reduced Ireland
"from a place of briskest trade and best paid rents in
Christendom to ruin and desolation," and who had
dared hold it for James Stuart, despite the Parliament
in London and the authority of the Prince of Orange,
was of Lord Baltimore's kin and his very close friend;
and Maryland teemed as no other colony did with Ro-

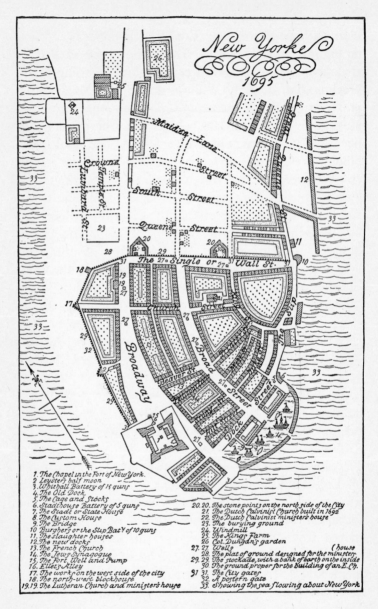

New Yorke
1695

1. The Chapel in the Fort of New York.
2. Leysler's half moon
3. Whitehall Battery of 15 guns
4. The Old Dock
5. The Cage and Stocks
6. Stadthouse Battery of 5 guns
7. The Stadt or State House
8. The Custom House
9. The Bridge
10. Burghers or the Slip Batt.y of 10 guns
11. The slaughter houses
12. The new docks
13. The French Church
14. The Jews Synagogue
15. The Fort, Well and Pump
16. Ellet's Alley
17. The works on the west side of the city
18. The north-west blockhouse
19.19. The Lutheran Church and minister's house

20.20. The stone points on the north side of the City
21. The Dutch Calvinist Church built in 1692
22. The Dutch Calvinist minister's house
23. The burying ground
24. Windmill
25. The Kings Farm
26. Col. Dungan's garden
27.27. Wells
28. The plat of ground designed for the minister's house
29.29. The stockade, with a bank of earth on the inside
30. The ground proper for the building of an E. Ch.
31.31. The City gates
32. A postern gate
33. Showing the sea flowing about New York

MAP OF NEW YORK IN 1695

man Catholic partisans. Lord Baltimore was, in fact, no laggard in his loyalty. He promptly despatched instructions out of England commanding the immediate proclamation of King William and Queen Mary to the province; but his messenger died on the way. and Maryland seemed to lag behind the other colonies in her loyalty. Upon which one John Coode, and some others, pretending, perhaps believing, that the proprietor's officers in the colony meant to defy the crown and establish papacy, got together an "Association in Arms for the Defence of the Protestant religion, and for asserting the right of King William and Queen Mary to the Province of Maryland and all the English dominions," officers of the militia and the very Speaker of the colonial House acting with them; seized the government of the colony (1689); convinced the King of their sincerity and good faith in what had been done, though many of the best people in the colony protested; ruled as their party pleased for two years; and then welcomed a royal governor (1692). They had made Maryland a royal province out of hand. Lord Baltimore was henceforth to receive only his quit-rents and the proceeds of the export duties.

It was a Protestant revolution with a vengeance. Taxes were ordered levied for the support of the Church of England. The immigration of Roman Catholics was prohibited and the public celebration of the mass forbidden by law. The seat of government was removed from St. Mary's, where the Catholic families held sway to whom the colony had owed its establishment, and set up at Providence, presently to be known as Annapolis, where the Protestant influence centred, Maryland was transformed.

339

Everywhere in the colonies there was doubt for a little while what government to obey, until things should be settled in England, and his Majesty King William should have time to turn his attention to affairs in America. Nowhere was the doubt more embarrassing than in East and West Jersey, which seemed left without any general government at all. Formal negotiations had been afoot in 1688, the very year of the revolution, for the surrender of the rights of the East Jersey proprietors to the crown; repeated transfers of proprietorship and redivisions of jurisdiction, both by private sale and public grant, had from the first sadly confused authority in the province; and when news came of what had happened in England, some doubted whether there were either royal authority or private right for the government of the growing hamlets of either colony. Affairs presently settled even there, however, to their normal frame again. For quite fourteen years longer the proprietors kept their right to appoint governors and exercise superintendence there. The settlers in the two provinces, moreover, were for the most part hard-headed English and Scottish people, who were not to be disconcerted in the management of their own affairs by trouble in England or the mere lack of a settled general government. For quite three years (1689–1692) they waited, without disturbance or excitement or any unusual interruption of their quiet life, under the direction of their town and county officers; until at last they learned what their government as a province was to be. There were already five organized counties in East Jersey, and had been these twenty years, since before the second coming of the Dutch (1674); and ten thousand people crowded their little towns and the cleared spaces of the forest about them. West Jersey, on the other side of the forests, by the Delaware, had grown almost as fast. Both provinces had the means and the men to take care of themselves.

It was not very long, after all, before government became a settled and ordered power again under the new King. William of Orange was a businesslike master, a real governor, not likely to do less, likely, rather, to do more, than either James or Charles in the government of the colonies; and the colonies felt the power of his systematic way of rule very soon. The old charters of Connecticut and Rhode Island were presently recognized again and confirmed; but Massachusetts, instead of her old, got a new charter. Plymouth lost her separate rights altogether and was merged with Massachusetts; and many things were changed. It must have seemed to the older men in the towns of the Plymouth grant as if the old freedom and dignity of their life had been done away with forever. Plymouth was the oldest of the northern colonies, and had kept through all the long seventy years of her separate life not a little of the fine temper, the sober resoluteness, steadfastness, moderation, and nobility given to her at the first by her pilgrim founders. Surely the King's advisers had forgotten her story when they thus summarily and without compunction handed her government and territory over to Massachusetts, to be, as it were, obliterated and robbed of their identity! But such, it seemed, was their way of bringing system into the administration of the northern colonies.

The new charter was granted in 1691. It not only joined Plymouth to Massachusetts, but Maine also, carrying the northern borders of the province to the very banks of the St. Lawrence. But, though it extended her boundaries, it curtailed her liberties, and it was this that the men of the Bay principally noted.

William Phips   SIR WILLIAM PHIPS

Their governor was thenceforth to be appointed by the crown. There were to be courts of admiralty, customs officers, and a post-office service directly dependent upon the ministers in London. There was to be a representative General Court, almost as before, consisting of the governor, his council, and a house of deputies, and the governor's council of twenty-eight was to be every year, after the first, elected by the General Court itself, in which the people's representatives predominated. Only the General Court could lay taxes and make general laws. But the King's governor was to have the right to veto any law of which he did not approve, and the crown behind him might set the Court's enactments aside, as disallowed, at any time within three years after they were passed. All the old rules as to who should vote for deputies, too, were changed. The right to vote was no longer to be confined to members of the Puritan churches; it was to be exercised by every man who had forty pounds' worth of personal property, or a freehold estate in land worth two pounds a year. Judges were to be appointed by the governor and council; all other officials of the colony by the governor alone.

It was something to have one of their own fellow colonists, a familiar figure among them, at least, for their first governor under the new arrangement, though that did not alter his powers, and he was hardly the man they would themselves have chosen. Sir William Phips was only a rough, pushing, self-made sailor, one of the youngest of the twenty-one sons of an humble gunsmith in a little settlement close by the mouth of the far-away Kennebec. He had been a ship's carpenter, a common seaman, a ship's captain,—always sanguine, always adventurous, always on the make, risking everything to win his way, and as cheerful and hearty and full of confident plans when he had lost as when he had won. At last he had actually made the fortune he was in quest of, by finding and recover-

PHIPS RECOVERING THE SUNKEN TREASURE

ing the treasure of a sunken Spanish galleon in the southern seas. He had been much in England, and had won favor in the court and out of it by his bluff and honest energy and unfailing good - will, and his breezy manners, brought fresh from the salt seas. King James had knighted him Sir William for the Spanish treasure he brought into England, and had made him high sheriff of New England when Sir Edmund Andros was governor there. In the year 1690, the year before the new charter was signed, he had led an expedition into the north and taken Acadia from the French, with much excellent private plunder, and then had failed in an expedition against Quebec. He was no statesman, and it was not pleasant for any man to be the first governor under the new charter; but bluff Sir William, known to every man in Boston, was better than a stranger might have been.

The new King's coming to the throne in England had brought war in its train, a long war with the French, as every one had foreseen it must,—"King William's War," they called it in the colonies; and war with the French meant fear and massacre on the northern borders, where the French were but too apt at stirring the Indians to their fierce attacks even in times of peace. It was this war Jacob Leisler had heard would surely bring French ships into New York and a Roman Catholic government. It gave Sir William Phips leave to make his expeditions against the north, for adventure and profit, instead.

In 1692 a distemper showed itself at Salem, in Massachusetts, which seemed for a little blacker than war itself,—an ominous distemper of the mind. It was the year of frenzy against what men fancied to be witch-craft, and Salem, where the chief madness was, saw nineteen persons swing upon her gallows hill for commerce with the devil. Some really believed them witches; some schemed to send their personal enemies to the gallows with a false charge. Governor Phips was induced to appoint special courts for the trial of the witches; and a long year went by before men's better thoughts,

WILLIAM PENN'S RESIDENCE IN 1699

natural pity, and awakened consciences called a halt upon the murderous frenzy, and Salem, with all the province, tried to forget what had been done to the innocent.

In that year, 1692, the King appointed Benjamin Fletcher to be governor of New York, and of Pennsylvania as well, which he was instructed to bring within his jurisdiction, for the consolidation of government; and Sir Lionel Copley, appointed in 1691, became royal

AN INTERVIEW BETWEEN SIR EDMUND ANDROS AND JAMES BLAIR

governor of Maryland. Sir Edmund Andros, too, was that year once more commissioned governor, this time of Virginia, and stayed there full five years, a quieter if not a wiser man than in the days of King James. The Virginians did not wholly dislike him, taking him for what he was, a rough soldier, more efficient than patient, who meant to do his duty according to his instructions, but did not know how to do it in the wise way for his own interests and the general peace. He honestly devoted himself to the welfare of the colony, encouraged the growth of cotton in order that cloth might be made, improved the methods of administration, and sought in more than one way to better the sources of wealth. But the Virginians liked as little as the other colonists did his zeal in the enforcement of the acts of trade; and his arbitrary temper ruined him at last by bringing him into collision with James Blair.

Andros's predecessor in the governorship of Virginia had been Francis Nicholson, a man who had been hardly more than a tool of James's tyranny a little while before in New York, but who was at heart something better than a mere placeman. He was intemperate, and in private often showed himself gross and licentious; but he had some of the gifts of a statesman, and in quiet Virginia devoted himself very steadily to the welfare of the people he governed, no less than to the advancement of the general interests of the crown. James Blair had found in him an intelligent friend, and not an opponent, when he sought to set up a college in the colony. A great deal of Virginian politics centred in Mr. Blair. He was a Scotsman bred to orders in the English Church, and was but thirty-six when Sir Edmund Andros was made governor of Virginia. He had come to the colony in 1685, at twenty-nine; and in 1690, the year Mr. Nicholson became governor, he had been appointed commissary for Virginia by the Bishop of London. Virginia was supposed to lie within the see of London, and as the bishop's commissary there it was Mr. Blair's duty to inspect, report upon, and administer discipline in the church of the colony. He

THE FIRST CHURCH IN NEWARK, NEW JERSEY

made it his first task to establish a college,—the assembly, the governor, and every true friend of Virginia at his back in the enterprise, — in order that education might sustain order and enlightenment. The King granted a charter and revenues to the college in 1692; the merchants of London subscribed right handsomely; Governor Nicholson handed over to it three hundred and fifty pounds voted to him by the assembly; and Virginia at last had the college she had wished and planned for ever since the days of Sir George Yeardley. It was agreed that it should be called the College of William and Mary.

But when Sir Edmund Andros came, Mr. Nicholson being sent to administer the affairs of Maryland, it was found, after a few years' trial, that he and Mr. Blair could not live in the same colony. Mr. Blair was as hot-tempered as Sir Edmund, and spoke his mind in as choleric and unstinted a way. But Mr. Blair, though he was often boisterous, generally managed, after the canny Scots manner, to be right as well, and generally had both the law and the interests of the colony on his side when it came to a contest, while Sir Edmund had a great talent for putting himself in the wrong. When at last it came to a breach between the two, therefore, as it did, Sir Edmund lost and Mr. Blair won. Sir Edmund was recalled to England, and Mr. Nicholson was named governor once more. It was a long time before Mr. Blair ceased to reign in Virginia. Mr. Nicholson became instrumental in removing the capital from Jamestown, which Mr. Bacon had burned, to Williamsburg, more wholesomely placed, ten miles back from the river. The college also had been placed there; and there Mr. Blair continued to preside as governors came and went.

For the *authorities* and *sources* for this period, see the references under Sections I. to V. and VII. to IX. of this chapter, so far as they cover the later years of the seventeenth century.

Wisconsin State College at Eau Claire
LIBRARY RULES

No book should be taken from the library until it has been properly charged by the librarian.

Books may be kept one week but are not to be renewed without special permission of the librarian.

A fine of two cents a day will be charged for books kept over time.

In case of loss or injury the person borrowing this book will be held responsible for a part or the whole of the value of a new book.

Due	DUE	Due	DUE